BASIC
COOKING

BASIC COOKING

NORMA MACMILLAN

Sebastian Kelly

This paperback edition published by
SEBASTIAN KELLY
2 Rectory Road
Oxford OX4 1BW

Produced by Anness Publishing Limited
Hermes House, 88-89 Blackfriars Road, London SE1 8HA

A CIP catalogue record for this book is available from the British Library

ISBN 1 84081 187 0

Publisher: Joanna Lorenz
Senior Cookery Editor: Linda Fraser
In House Editor: Anne Hildyard
Copy Editors: Jane Sigal and Penny David
Designers: Sheila Volpe and Sîan Keugh
Jacket Designer: Adrian Morris
Photographer: Amanda Heywood
Food Styling: Elizabeth Wolf-Cohen,
steps by Marilyn Forbes and Cara Hobday

Printed In Singapore by Star Standard Industries Pte. Ltd.

The author would like to thank Jill Eggleton
for her help in testing recipes.

Previously published as part of a larger compendium,
The Cook's Kitchen Bible.

© Anness Publishing Limited 1996
Updated © 1999
1 3 5 7 9 10 8 6 4 2

CONTENTS

~

~ Introduction ~

Whether you are a complete novice, an experienced cook, or an occasional dabbler, there are times when everyone longs for basic techniques and methods to be laid out clearly and simply. This book does just that.

In addition, there are lots of recipes and recipe ideas, too, so you can try out the skills you are learning or brushing up. The recipes are designed to illustrate a particular technique. When you read these recipes, take a moment to assess any additional techniques required. Look them up in the index, if you want to review.

USEFUL EQUIPMENT

To be able to cook efficiently and with pleasure, you need good equipment. That is not to say that you should invest in an extensive collection of pots, pans, tools, and gadgets, but a basic range of cookware is essential.

In addition, buy the best equipment you can afford, adding more as your budget allows. Well made equipment lasts and is a sound investment; inexpensive cookware is likely to dent, break, or develop "hot spots" where food will stick and burn, so will need replacing. Flimsy tools will make food preparation more time consuming and frustrating.

For the Rangetop

When choosing pots and pans, look for those with heavy bases, sturdy insulated handles and knobs, and tight-fitting lids. Bear in mind, too, how much the pan will weigh when full – a large pot for pasta or stock must not be too heavy for you to lift.

Copper conducts heat best, but is hard to care for. Aluminum is good, as is cast iron, although the latter needs scrupulous care to prevent rust. Enamel- or porcelain-coated cast iron is a good compromise. Stainless steel is lightweight and durable, but it conducts heat unevenly. A composite or clad bottom containing another metal can improve heat conduction.

- **Rangetop essentials**: 3 saucepans with lids (1-, 2-, and 3-quart), 6- or 8-inch skillet, 12-inch skillet with lid, flameproof casserole or Dutch oven with lid (4- or 6-quart), kettle or stockpot with lid (8-quart).
- **Helpful equipment**: Double boiler, wok, omelette pan, crêpe pan, sauté pan, ridged grill pan, steamer.

For the Oven

Cake and muffin pans and baking sheets should be made of shiny metal (aluminum, tin, or stainless steel) for even heat distribution. Pie plates should be dull metal, ceramic, or glass. Roasting pans can be made of any material, but they must be sturdy, as should all bakeware.

- **Baking and roasting essentials**: 9-inch round cake pans, 8- or 9-inch square cake pans, 9- × 13-inch baking pan, loaf pan (8- × 4-inch or 9- × 5-inch, or both), muffin pan, 9-inch pie plate, 9-inch removable bottom tart pan, 9-inch springform pan, 10- × 15-inch jelly roll pan, 2 baking sheets, roasting pan with rack, wire rack, large soufflé dish, shallow and deep baking dishes, broiler pan with rack, pot holders or oven mitts, oven and meat thermometers.

- **Helpful bakeware**: 2 layer cake pans (8- or 9-inch), 10-inch tube pan, round and square pans, pie plates, tart pans, and springform pans of various sizes, individual soufflé dishes, gratin dishes, metal skewers.

Cutting Tools

A good set of knives is the most important tool in food preparation. Yet so many cooks make do with flimsy, dull, or nicked knives, which can turn even the chopping of onions into an arduous task.

Knives made of carbon steel can be given the sharpest edge, but they rust and discolor easily so must be washed and dried immediately after use. High-carbon stainless steel knives will take a sharp edge and they resist discoloration, but are more expensive. Ordinary stainless steel knives are very difficult to sharpen efficiently.

Whatever knives you choose, keep them sharp. More accidents occur with blunt knives than sharp ones.

- **Cutting essentials**: Chef's knife with rigid 10-inch blade, paring knife with rigid 3-inch blade, flexible vegetable knife with serrated edge and pointed tip, rigid serrated knife with 10- to 12-inch blade, sturdy kitchen scissors, knife block or magnetized bar, several cutting boards in different sizes and reserved for different uses.
- **Helpful cutting tools**: Filleting knife with thin flexible 7-inch blade and sharp point, boning knife with thin rigid 6-inch blade, utility knife with rigid 6-inch blade, grapefruit knife with curved serrated blade, poultry shears, carving knife and fork.

Preparation Tools

You can do a lot with just a big bowl and a sturdy spoon, but there are many tools that make cooking easier.

● **Preparation essentials**: 4 mixing bowls in varying sizes, wooden spoons, long-handled slotted spoon, ladle, wooden spatula, rubber spatulas, narrow metal spatula with flexible 10-inch blade, slotted spatula/pancake turner, tongs, 12-inch wire balloon whisk, handheld electric mixer, citrus press, colander, measuring cups (liquid and dry) and spoons, vegetable peeler, grater, 2 strainers (1 metal, 1 nylon), 2-pronged fork, rolling pin, pastry brush, can and bottle openers, corkscrew, kitchen timer, paper towels, wraps, string.

● **Helpful equipment**: Salad spinner, food processor and/or blender, potato ricer, meat pounder, rotary grater, nutmeg grater, citrus zester, channeling knife, apple corer, melon baller, pastry blender, pastry scraper, trussing needle, cherry pitter, pasta machine, countertop electric mixer, parchment paper.

BUYING AND STORING FOOD

A well-stocked kitchen makes meal preparation easy. The key is planning – planning menus for the next few days or the week ahead, then making a shopping list that includes fresh foods as well as those frequently-used foods whose stocks are running low or that are near or past their expiration date. Allow yourself to be a little flexible, though. When shopping, take advantage of fresh seasonal foods and special offers.

Knowing how and where to store food – both fresh and preserved – and how long to keep it will be a great help in shopping to stock the kitchen.

In the Refrigerator

All foods in the refrigerator or freezer should be well wrapped or stored in sealed containers. This preserves flavor and moisture, and prevents the flavors and odors of other, stronger foods being transferred. It is essential to keep raw meat and poultry well wrapped as their drippings can transfer bacteria to other foods.

Perishable fresh foods, such as meats, poultry, fish and seafood, eggs, cheese and other dairy products, and many fruits and vegetables, must be kept refrigerated at a temperature of 35–40°F. For longer storage, many can also be frozen at 0°F or lower. Cooked leftovers must also be refrigerated or frozen. Check the refrigerator and freezer temperatures with a special thermometer. If temperatures are too high, food will spoil rapidly.

Storing Fresh Fruits

Those fruits that can be kept at room temperature while still unripe include apricots, kiwi fruits, mangoes,

nectarines, papayas, peaches, pears, pineapples, and plums. Once ripe, all these should be refrigerated and eaten within 2–3 days.

Fruits that can be stored at cool room temperature include apples (although they will be crisper if refrigerated), bananas, dates, lemons, limes, grapefruit, and oranges. Apples can be kept at room temperature for a few days, dates for several weeks, and citrus fruit up to a week; beyond that, refrigerate them.

Unless you intend to eat them on the day of purchase, refrigerate fully ripe and perishable fresh fruits. These include berries, cherries, figs, grapes, melons, pomegranates, and tangerines. They can be kept refrigerated for 2–3 days.

Storing Fresh Vegetables

Like fruits, there are some vegetables that can stored at room temperature. A dark, cool place (about 50°F) with good ventilation is ideal. Suitable vegetables are chayotes, garlic, onions, potatoes and sweet potatoes, rutabaga, and winter squash. All can be kept about 2 months. Store tomatoes at room temperature until they are ripe. After that, refrigerate.

Perishable vegetables should be refrigerated. Some, such as peas or corn should be used quickly, while others, like carrots or cabbage, can be kept for a longer period. In most cases, do not wash the vegetable until just before using. Celery, curly endive, escarole, hearty greens, herbs, lettuce, spinach and watercress should be washed before storage.

Storing Canned and Dry Foods

Full pantry shelves are a boon for a busy cook, but canned and dry foods can deteriorate if not stored properly or if left too long on the shelf. Kitchen cabinets should be cool (no more than 65°F) and dry. Staples such as flour, salt, sugar, pasta, and grains are best stored in moistureproof containers. If necessary remove them from their wrappings and decant them into canisters or jars. Whole-grain products (whole-wheat flour and pasta, brown rice, etc.) cannot be kept as long as refined ones.

Dried herbs and spices will keep their flavor and scent best if stored in sealed jars. Light is their enemy; store in a cabinet or drawer, rather than on an open spice rack. Oil, too, should be stored in a cool dark place, in an airtight container. Refrigerate nut oils to preserve them longer.

Herbs and Spices

The judicious use of an herb or spice, or both, can transform a dish. It's fun to experiment, once you know what you like and which seasonings go well with what foods.

Whenever possible, use fresh herbs, for their wonderful flavor, scent, and color. They're widely available in supermarkets and are also easy to grow, even in pots on a windowsill. Fresh herbs impart their flavor very quickly, so chop just before using, and add to hot dishes towards the end of cooking. If fresh herbs are not available, you can, of course, substitute dried. Use them in a ratio of 1 teaspoon dried to 1 tablespoon fresh.

Most spices, both whole and ground, need time to impart their aroma and flavor to a dish. Some are pungent and spicy-hot, others are sweet and fragrant. If you can, grind spices freshly, using a spice mill, nutmeg grater, or mortar and pestle. The difference in flavor and aroma between pre-ground and freshly ground is amazing.

GETTING THE TIMING RIGHT

Successful meal preparation is as much dependent on organization as on culinary skills. The initial planning of a menu – whether for the family supper or a company dinner – must give consideration to many things: a good range of flavors, colors, and textures, as well as a balance in protein, fat, fiber, and other healthy considerations.

That done, it then becomes a question of what you can prepare ahead, and what remains to do at the last minute so that all is ready at the same time. For the beginner, this can be daunting.

The first step is to read all the recipes before making a final choice. The main dish, with simple accompaniments such as vegetables or a salad and bread, is a good starting point. Surround that with a cold first course (if there is to be one) and a cold dessert that can be made ahead of time. This way you can concentrate your efforts at each stage.

If you do choose two or more hot dishes, consider their cooking times and oven temperatures. If you have only one oven, and the temperatures required for the two dishes are different, this will present difficulties.

Next, make a shopping list. Check that you have all the equipment you require. Once you have everything on hand, you can start the preparation.

Read each recipe through again so you know what lies ahead and try to estimate how long each preparation stage will take. Review techniques in the preparation that are unfamiliar, using the index to locate them, if necessary. Set the time you want to serve the meal, and work back from there so you know when to start the preparation. It's not a bad idea to write down all these times, as if you were planning military strategy.

If you are serving a first course, you will need to plan what can be left unattended while you are at the table. If your chosen dessert is frozen, it may need some time out of the freezer before serving, so decide at what point to transfer it to the refrigerator.

Remember to allow time for the final draining of vegetables, or carving of meat, or seasoning of a sauce. It is usually the case that all of these need to be done at the same time – but you only have one pair of hands. So decide what can wait and what will keep hot. Also allow time for plates to be cleared from the table if you are serving more than one course.

If any recipe requires the oven to be preheated or pans to be prepared, do this first. Pots of boiling salted water for cooking vegetables or pasta can be brought to the boil while you are doing the chopping and slicing.

Set out all the ingredients required and prepare them according to recipe directions. If more than one dish calls for the same ingredients, say chopped onion or parsley, you can prepare the total amount at the same time.

Now start cooking, following your timetable. Check the recipe as you work, and don't be distracted. Keep tasting and sniffing the food as you go – that's much of the fun!

MEASURING TECHNIQUES

Cooks with years of experience, preparing familiar recipes, may not need to measure ingredients, but if you are a beginning cook or are trying a new recipe for the first time, it is a good idea to follow instructions carefully. Also, measuring all the ingredients precisely will insure consistent results.

The recipes in this book have been tested using a conventional, not fan assisted, oven. Unless specified otherwise, flour is all-purpose, sugar is granulated, and eggs are USDA size large.

SOME USEFUL EQUIVALENTS

3 teaspoons = 1 tablespoon = ½ fluid ounce = 14.79 milliliters

4 tablespoons = ¼ cup = 2 fluid ounces

5 tablespoons + 1 teaspoon = ⅓ cup

8 tablespoons = ½ cup = 4 fluid ounces

10 tablespoons + 2 teaspoons = ⅔ cup

12 tablespoons = ¾ cup = 6 fluid ounces

16 tablespoons = 1 cup = 8 fluid ounces = 236.6 milliliters

2 cups = 1 pint = 16 fluid ounces

4 cups or 2 pints = 1 quart = 32 fluid ounces

1.06 quarts = 1 liter

4 quarts = 1 gallon = 128 fluid ounces

---

1 ounce = 28.35 grams

16 ounces = 1 pound = 453.59 grams

2.205 pounds = 1 kilogram

---

1 inch = 2.5 centimeters

12 inches = 1 foot = 30 centimeters/.305 meter

40 inches = 3.28 feet = 1 meter

1 ▲ For liquids measured in cups: Use a glass or clear plastic measuring cup. Put the cup on a flat surface and pour in the liquid. Bend down and check that the liquid is exactly level with the marking on the cup, as specified in the recipe.

3 ▲ For measuring dry ingredients in a cup or spoon: Fill the cup or spoon. Level the surface even with the rim of the cup or spoon, using the straight edge of a knife.

5 ▲ For measuring brown sugar in a cup or spoon: If the recipe specifies firmly packed brown sugar, scoop the sugar and press it firmly into the cup or spoon. Level the surface.

2 ▲ For liquids measured in spoons: Pour the liquid into the measuring spoon, to the brim, and then pour it into the mixing bowl. Do not hold the spoon over the bowl when measuring because liquid may overflow.

4 ▲ For measuring flour in a cup or spoon: Scoop the flour from the canister in the measuring cup or spoon. Hold it over the canister and level the surface.

6 ▲ For measuring butter: With a sharp knife, cut off the specified amount following the markings on the wrapper.

POULTRY & MEAT

~

Poultry is always popular and this chapter helps you make the most of it. Clearly explained preparation and cooking techniques show how simple it is to roast, stew and pan-fry meat, as well as make great gravy and superb stock.

ROASTING POULTRY

Where would family gatherings be without the time-honored roasted bird? But beyond the favorite chicken, all types of poultry can be roasted – from small Cornish hens to large turkeys. However, older, tougher birds are better pot-roasted.

Protect and Flavor

Before roasting, loosen the skin on the breast by gently easing it away from the flesh with your fingers. Press in softened butter – mixed with herbs or garlic for extra flavor – and smooth back the skin.

Simple Roast Chicken

Squeeze the juice from a halved lemon over a 3- to 3½-pound chicken, then push the lemon halves into the body cavity. Smear 1 tablespoon softened butter over the breast. Roast in a preheated 375°F oven until done, about 1¼ hours. Skim all fat from the roasting juices, then add ½ cup water and bring to a boil, stirring well to mix in the browned bits. Season with salt and pepper, and pass this sauce with the chicken. *Serves 4.*

1 ▲ Wipe the bird inside and out with damp paper towels. Stuff the bird, if the recipe directs, and truss it. Spread the breast of chicken with melted or softened butter or oil; bard the breast of a lean game bird; prick the skin of duck and goose.

3 ▲ Roast the bird, basting it every 10 minutes after the first ½ hour with the juices and fat in the pan. Turn it if the recipe directs. If it is browning too quickly, cover loosely with foil.

2 ▲ Set the bird breast-up on a rack in a small roasting pan or shallow baking dish. If you are roasting a lean game bird, set the bird in the pan breast down.

4 ▲ Transfer the bird to a carving board and let it rest at least 15 minutes. If desired, deglaze for a simple pan sauce or make gravy with the pan juices.

ROASTING TIMES FOR POULTRY

Note: Cooking times given here are for unstuffed birds. For stuffed birds, add 20 minutes to the total roasting time.

Cornish hen	1–1½ pounds	1–1¼ hours at 350°F
Chicken (broiler-fryer or roaster)	2½–3 pounds	1–1¼ hours at 375°F
	3½–4 pounds	1¼–1¾ hours at 375°F
	4½–5 pounds	1½–2 hours at 375°F
	5–6 pounds	1¾–2½ hours at 375°F
Capon	5–7 pounds	1¾–2 hours at 325°F
Duck (domestic)	3–5 pounds	1¾–2¼ hours at 400°F
Goose	8–10 pounds	2½–3 hours at 350°F
	10–12 pounds	3–3½ hours at 350°F
Turkey (whole bird)	6–8 pounds	3–3½ pounds at 325°F
	8–12 pounds	3–4 hours at 325°F
	12–16 pounds	4–5 hours at 325°F
Turkey (whole breast)	4–6 pounds	1½–2¼ hours at 325°F
	6–8 pounds	2¼–3¼ hours at 325°F

Cornish Hens Waldorf

SERVES 6

6 Cornish hens, each weighing about 1¼ pounds

3–4 tablespoons melted butter

FOR THE STUFFING

2 tablespoons butter

1 onion, minced

2 cups cooked rice

2 celery stalks, minced

2 red-skinned apples, cored and finely diced

½ cup chopped walnuts

⅓ cup cream sherry or apple cider

2 tablespoons lemon juice

salt and pepper

1 Preheat the oven to 350°F.

2 For the stuffing, melt the butter in a small frying pan and fry the onion, stirring occasionally, until soft. Turn the onion and butter into a bowl and add the remaining stuffing ingredients. Season with salt and pepper and mix well.

3 ◀ Divide the stuffing among the hens, stuffing the body cavities. Truss the hens. Arrange in a roasting pan. Sprinkle with salt and pepper and drizzle over the melted butter.

4 Roast until cooked through, 1¼–1½ hours. Untruss before serving.

CARVING POULTRY

Carving a bird neatly for serving makes the presentation attractive. You will need a sharp, long-bladed knife, or an electric knife, plus a long, 2-pronged fork and a carving board with a well to catch the juices.

Cut away any trussing string. For a stuffed bird, spoon the stuffing from the cavity into a serving bowl. For easier carving, remove the wishbone.

Insert the fork into one breast to hold the bird steady. Cut through the skin to the leg joint on that side of the body, then slice through the joint to sever the leg from the body. Repeat on the other side.

1 ▲ Slice through the joint in each leg to sever the thigh and drumstick. If carving turkey, slice the meat off the thigh and drumstick, parallel to the bone, turning to get even slices; leave thighs and drumsticks of chicken whole.

2 ▲ To carve the breast meat of a turkey or chicken, cut ⅛–¼-inch thick slices at an angle, slicing down on both sides of the breastbone. For smaller birds, remove the meat on each side of the breastbone in a single piece, then slice across.

TRUSSING POULTRY

Trussing holds a bird together during cooking so that it keeps a neat, attractive shape. If the bird is stuffed, trussing prevents the stuffing from falling out. You can truss with strong string or with poultry skewers or lacers as shown here.

Alternatively, use a long trussing needle and string. Pass the needle through the body from one side to the other near where the legs are attached, then through both wings and tie the string. Pass the needle through the tail and tie the string around the ends of the drumsticks.

Remove all trussing before serving.

1 ▲ For an unstuffed bird: Set it breast down and pull the flap of neck skin over the neck opening. Turn the bird onto its back. Fold each wing tip back, over the neck skin, to secure firmly behind the shoulder.

2 ▲ Cross the ends of the drumsticks and press the legs firmly down and into the breast.

3 ▲ If there is a band of skin across the tail, tuck the ends of the drumsticks under the skin. Otherwise, loop a length of string several times around the drumstick ends, then tie a knot and trim off excess string.

4 ▲ For a stuffed bird: Fold the wing tips back as above. If the bird has been stuffed in the neck end, first fold the flap of skin over the opening and secure it with a skewer, then fold over the wing tips.

5 ▲ Put any stuffing or flavorings (herbs, lemon halves, apple or onion quarters, etc.) in the body cavity, then secure the ends of the drumsticks as above, tying in the tail end, too.

6 ▲ Alternatively, the cavity opening can be closed with skewers: Insert 2 or more skewers across the opening, threading them through the skin several times.

7 ▲ Lace the skewers together with string. Tie the drumsticks together over the skewers.

Stuffing Tips
- Stuffing should be cool, not hot or chilled when put into the bird.
- Pack it loosely in the bird because it expands during cooking. Cook any leftover stuffing separately in a baking dish.
- Do not stuff poultry until just before cooking.
- If stuffing the body cavity of a large bird, use maximum roasting times because the stuffing could inhibit heat penetration, and thus not kill all harmful bacteria.

CUTTING UP POULTRY

Although chickens and other poultry are sold already cut up, sometimes it makes sense to buy a whole bird and to disjoint it yourself. That way you can prepare 4 larger pieces or 8 smaller ones, depending on the recipe, and you can cut the pieces so that the backbone and other bony bits (which can be saved for stock) are not included. Also a whole bird is cheaper to buy than pieces.

A sharp knife and sturdy kitchen scissors or poultry shears make the job of cutting up a chicken very easy.

1 ▲ With a knife, cut through the skin on one side of the body down to the leg joint. Bend the leg out away from the body and twist it to break the hip joint.

2 ▲ Hold the leg out away from the body and cut through the joint, taking the "oyster" meat from the backbone with the leg. Repeat the same procedure on the other side to remove the other leg.

Safe Handling of Raw Poultry
Raw poultry may harbor potentially harmful organisms, such as salmonella bacteria, so it is important to take care in its preparation. Always wash your hands, the chopping board, knife, and poultry shears in hot soapy water before and after handling the poultry. It is best to use a chopping board that can be washed at high temperature in a dishwasher and, if possible, to keep the chopping board just for the preparation of raw poultry. Also, make sure to thaw frozen poultry completely before cooking.

3 ▲ To separate the breast from the back, cut through the flap of skin just below the rib cage, cutting toward the neck. Pull the breast and back apart and cut through the joints that connect them on each side. Reserve the back for stock.

4 ▲ Turn the whole breast over, skin side down. Take one side of the breast in each hand and bend back firmly so the breastbone pops free. Loosen the bone on both sides with your fingers and, with the help of the knife, remove it.

5 ▲ Cut the breast lengthwise in half, cutting through the wishbone. You now have 2 breast halves with wings attached and 2 leg portions.

6 ▲ For 8 pieces, cut each breast half in half at an angle so that some breast meat is included with a wing portion. Trim off any protruding bones.

7 ▲ With the knife, cut each leg portion through the joint to separate the thigh and drumstick.

PAN-BRAISING POULTRY

Pan-braising combines frying and braising, producing particularly succulent results. It is a method suitable for pieces of poultry as well as for small whole birds such as quails, squab chickens, and Cornish hens.

As with frying, the poultry should be dried thoroughly with paper towels before cooking to ensure that it browns quickly and evenly.

1 ▲ Heat a little oil, a mixture of oil and butter, or clarified butter in a heavy frying pan or sauté pan.

2 ▲ Add the poultry and fry it over medium-high heat until it is deep golden brown all over.

3 ▲ Add liquid and flavorings as directed in the recipe. Bring to a boil, then cover and reduce the heat to medium-low. Continue cooking gently until the poultry is done, turning the pieces or birds once or twice for even cooking.

4 ▲ If the recipe directs, remove the poultry from the pan and keep it warm while finishing the sauce. This can be as simple as boiling the cooking juices to reduce them, or adding butter or cream for a richer result.

5 ▲ **To thicken cooking juices**: Mash equal parts of butter and flour to a paste (called "beurre manié"). Use 1 tablespoon each of butter and flour to thicken 1 cup of liquid. Whisk small pieces gradually into the boiling sauce until it is smooth and silky.

6 ▲ Another method of thickening cooking juices is to add a mixture of cornstarch and water (2 teaspoons cornstarch diluted with 1 tablespoon water per cup of cooking liquid). Boil for 2–3 minutes, whisking constantly, until the sauce is syrupy.

Pan-Braised Chicken with Bacon and Mushrooms
Chop 6 slices bacon and cook over medium heat until lightly colored. Remove and reserve. Pour off most of the fat. Dredge a 3½-pound chicken, cut in 8 pieces, in seasoned flour. Fry in the remaining fat, turning, until golden. Add 3 tablespoons dry white wine and 1 cup poultry stock. Bring to a boil. Add 6 ounces mushrooms, quartered and browned in 1 tablespoon butter, and the bacon. Cover and cook over low heat until tender, 20–25 minutes. *Serves 4.*

FRYING CHICKEN

Fried chicken is justifiably popular – crisp and brown outside and tender and juicy within. It's a quick and easy cooking method that can be applied to pieces of rabbit and hare and small pieces of turkey, too.

Dry the pieces thoroughly with paper towels before frying. If they are at all wet, they will not brown properly. If the recipe directs, lightly coat or bread the pieces.

Succulent Fried Chicken
Lightly mix 1 cup milk with 1 beaten egg in a shallow dish. On a sheet of wax paper or in a plastic bag, combine 1 cup flour, 1 teaspoon paprika, salt, and pepper. One at a time, dip 8 chicken pieces in the egg mixture and turn them to coat all over. Then dip in the seasoned flour and shake off any excess. Deep-fry 25–30 minutes, turning the pieces so they brown and cook evenly. Drain on paper towels and serve very hot. *Serves 4.*

1 ▲ For pan-frying: Heat oil, a mixture of oil and butter, or clarified butter in a large, heavy-based frying pan over medium-high heat. When the oil is very hot, put in the chicken pieces, skin side down. Do not crowd them or they will not brown evenly; cook in batches if necessary.

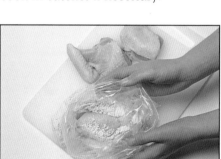

3 ▲ For deep-frying: Dip the pieces into a mixture of milk and beaten egg, then coat lightly with seasoned flour; let the coating set 20 minutes before frying. (Or, coat them with a batter just before frying.)

5 ▲ With a slotted metal spatula or tongs, lower the chicken pieces into the oil, a few at a time, without crowding them. Deep-fry until they are golden brown all over and cooked. Turn them so they color evenly.

2 ▲ Fry until deep golden brown all over, turning the pieces so they color evenly. Fry until all the chicken pieces are thoroughly cooked. Remove pieces of breast before drumsticks and thighs (dark meat takes longer to cook than white meat). Drain on paper towels.

4 ▲ Half fill a deep pan with vegetable oil and heat it to 365°F. You can also test the temperature with a cube of bread. Drop in the bread; if it takes 50 seconds to brown, the oil is at the right temperature.

6 ▲ Drain on paper towels and serve hot. If you want to keep a batch of fried chicken hot while you fry the rest, put it into a low oven, but don't cover it or it will become soggy.

PREPARING MEAT FOR COOKING

You can buy meat ready for cooking from butchers and most good supermarkets. However, some cuts need further preparation, depending on how they are to be cooked – removing excess fat or adding protective fat, for example, or tying a roast after stuffing.

How Much to Buy
As a general guide, when buying boneless meat that has little or no fat, allow 5–7 ounces per serving. For bone-in meat that has a little fat at the edge, allow about ½ pound per serving. Very bony cuts such as shank and spareribs have proportionally little meat so you will need 1 pound per serving.

1 ▲ To trim: If a recipe directs, use a sharp knife to trim all fat from the surface. Leave a little fat on steaks to be grilled, and slash this fat at regular intervals to prevent the steak curling up during cooking. Meat cuts to be roasted should retain a thin layer of fat (⅛–¼ inch). Cut away the sinews and tough connective tissue.

2 ▲ If you like, cut and scrape all fat and gristle from the ends of protruding bones (such as on chops or roasts that contain rib bones); this is called "frenching."

3 ▲ To chine a roast: For large cuts of meat that contain rib bones, such as beef rib roast, pork loin, and rack of lamb, it is a good idea to cut the chine bone (backbone) where it is joined to the rib bones, to loosen it, or to remove it completely before cooking. Do this with a meat saw and sharp knife. Without the chine bone, the roast will be easy to carve.

4 ▲ To bard a roast: If a very lean cut of meat is to be roasted without a protective crust (a spice mixture, oil and crumbs, or pastry, for example), it is a good idea to bard it to keep it moist. Wrap very thin slices of beef fat, pork fatback, or blanched bacon around the roast and tie them in place. Discard the fat before serving but keep the bacon, if desired.

5 ▲ To tie a boned roast: Cuts that have been boned should be tied into a neat shape for roasting or pot roasting. The butcher will do this, but if you want to add a stuffing or seasoning, you will need to retie the roast yourself. Reshape it into a neat roll that is even in circumference. Use butcher's twine to make ties around the circumference at 1-inch intervals.

Boned Pork Loin with Apple Cream Sauce

SERVES 6

3-pound boned pork loin roast, barded, rolled, and tied

1 tablespoon fresh thyme leaves, or 1 teaspoon dried thyme

salt and pepper

fresh thyme sprigs, watercress, and sliced apples, for garnishing

FOR THE SAUCE

1½ tablespoons butter

1 onion, chopped

2 apples, such as Granny Smiths, peeled, cored, and chopped

½ cup whipping cream

½ tablespoon Dijon-style mustard

1 tablespoon cream-style horseradish

1 Preheat the oven to 375°F.

2 ▲ Untie the pork loin and set the barding fat aside. Lay the pork out flat. Sprinkle it with the thyme, salt, and pepper and pat on.

~ **COOK'S TIP** ~

A boned roast will take longer to cook than the same weight roast with bone. This is because the bone conducts heat more readily than the flesh.

3 Reroll the loin and tie it into a neat shape, with the barding fat.

4 Put the pork loin on a rack in a small roasting pan. Roast until well cooked, about 1¼–1½ hours.

5 ▼ Meanwhile, for the sauce, melt the butter in a saucepan and add the onion and apples. Cook over low heat, stirring occasionally, until very soft, 20–25 minutes.

6 ▲ Let the apple mixture cool slightly, then transfer it to a food processor. Add the cream, mustard, and horseradish. Blend until smooth. Season with salt and pepper. Return the sauce to the pan and reheat just before serving.

7 When the pork is cooked, remove it from the oven and let it rest about 10 minutes before carving. Garnish with thyme, watercress, and apples.

ROASTING MEAT

The dry heat of oven-roasting is best suited to tender cuts of meat. If they don't have a natural marbling of fat, bard them. Alternatively, marinate the meat or baste it frequently with the roasting juices during cooking.

Meat for roasting should be at room temperature. Roast on a rack in a pan that is just a little larger than the roast. Without a rack, the base of the roast would stew and not become crisp.

There are two methods of roasting meat. For the first, the roast is seared at a high temperature and then the heat is reduced for the remainder of the cooking time. For the second method, the meat is roasted at a constant temperature throughout. Scientific studies have shown that both methods produce good results, and that it is prolonged cooking, not the method, that affects juiciness and shrinkage. So use whichever method you prefer or follow recipe directions.

Suggested Roasting Times
Following the second roasting method, in a 350°F oven, approximate timings in minutes per pound:
    Beef, rare, 20 + 20 extra*
          medium, 25 + 25 extra
          well done, 30 + 30 extra
    Veal, 25 + 25 extra
    Lamb, 25 + 25 extra
    Pork, 35 + 35 extra
(*Prime cuts such as rib of beef and tenderloin need less time.)

1 ▲ According to recipe directions, rub the roast with oil or butter and season. If desired, with the tip of a sharp knife, make little slits in the meat all over the surface. Insert flavorings such as herbs, slivers of garlic, olive slices, shards of fresh ginger, and so on.

2 ▲ Insert a meat thermometer in the thickest part, not touching a bone. (An instant-read thermometer is sometimes inserted toward the end of roasting.) Roast for the suggested time, basting if necessary, until the meat has reached the desired degree of doneness.

3 ▲ Transfer the meat to a carving board and let it rest for 10–15 minutes before carving. If desired, deglaze for a simple pan sauce or make gravy with the roasting juices.

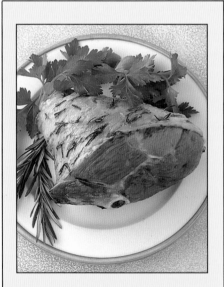

Roast Leg of Lamb
Trim a 6-pound bone-in leg of lamb, removing almost all the fat. Cut 2–3 garlic cloves into very thin slices. Pull the leaves from 3 sprigs of fresh rosemary. Insert the garlic slices and rosemary leaves in the slits in the lamb. Rub the lamb with olive oil and season with salt and pepper. Roast to the desired degree of doneness. *Serves 8.*

MEAT THERMOMETER READINGS

Beef		Lamb	
rare	125–130°F	rare	130–135°F
medium-rare	135°F	medium	140–145°F
medium	140–145°F	well done	160°F
well done	160°F		
		Pork	
Veal		medium	150°F
well done	160°F	well done	160–165°F

TESTING FOR DONENESS

The cooking times given in a recipe are intended to be a guideline. The shape of a cut can affect how long it takes to cook, and people have different preferences for how well cooked they like meat to be. So testing is essential.

Natural Law of Roasting
A roast will continue to cook in its own retained heat for 5–10 minutes after being removed from oven or pot, so it is a good idea to take it out when it has reached 5° short of the desired thermometer reading.

1 ▲ Large cuts of meat that are roasted or pot roasted can be tested with a metal skewer. Insert the skewer into the thickest part and leave it 30 seconds. Withdraw the skewer and feel it. If it is warm, the meat is rare; if it is hot, the meat is well cooked.

2 ▲ The most reliable test for doneness is with a meat thermometer, inserted in the center of the roast, away from bones. Some instant-read thermometers are inserted at the end of cooking. Follow manufacturer's instructions. See the chart for the internal temperatures.

COOKING METHODS AND CHOICE OF MEAT CUTS

Roasting
Beef: chuck eye roast, rib roast, rib eye roast, back ribs, tenderloin roast, top sirloin roast, sirloin tip roast, bottom round roast, top round roast, round tip roast, eye round roast
Veal: rib roast, shoulder roast, loin roast, breast roast
Pork: blade roast, loin roast, top loin roast, tenderloin, rib crown roast, spareribs, country-style ribs, back ribs, smoked picnic, smoked shoulder roll, smoked ham, country ham, smoked loin chop, Canadian bacon
Lamb: shoulder roast, rib roast, loin roast, leg, leg roast, spareribs

Pot-roasting, braising, and stewing
Beef: mock tender roast (chuck), top blade roast, shoulder pot roast, arm pot roast, short ribs, back ribs, round steak, bottom round roast, round tip roast, eye round roast, brisket (fresh and corned), shanks, flank steak, skirt steak
Veal: blade steak, shoulder steak and roast, rib chop, loin chop, sirloin steak, top round steak, cutlet, riblet, breast roast, shanks
Pork: shoulder roast, blade steak and roast, loin chop, top loin chop, rib chop, sirloin chop, spareribs, country-style ribs, back ribs, smoked picnic, smoked hock, smoked shoulder roll
Lamb: arm chop, shoulder roast, blade chop, sirloin chop, spareribs, shanks, riblets

Pan-frying
Beef: rib eye steak, top loin steak, tenderloin steak (filet mignon), T-bone steak, porterhouse steak, shell steak (Delmonico steak), sirloin steak, round tip steak, round steak, flank steak, skirt steak
Veal: blade steak, shoulder steak, rib chop, loin chop, sirloin steak, top round steak, cutlet
Pork: blade steak, loin chop, top loin chop, rib chop, sirloin chop, ham slice, smoked loin chop, Canadian bacon, bacon
Lamb: arm chop, blade chop, rib chop, loin chop, sirloin chop

Broiling and grilling
Beef: chuck steak, blade steak, rib steak, rib eye steak, top loin steak, tenderloin steak (filet mignon), T-bone steak, porterhouse steak, shell steak (Delmonico steak), sirloin steak, round tip steak, round steak, flank steak, skirt steak
Veal: rib chop, loin chop, sirloin steak, cutlet
Pork: blade steak, loin chop, top loin chop, rib chop, sirloin chop, spareribs, country-style ribs, back ribs, ham slice, smoked loin chop, Canadian bacon, bacon
Lamb: arm chop, blade chop, rib chop, loin chop, sirloin chop, butterflied leg, leg steaks, spareribs, riblets

Stir-frying
Beef: flank steak, skirt steak, mock tender (chuck)
Veal: top round steak, cutlet
Pork: tenderloin
Lamb: sirloin, leg

MAKING GRAVY

Gravy made from the roasting juices is rich in flavor and color. It is a traditional accompaniment for roast meat and poultry.

For a thinner sauce, an alternative method to that explained here is deglazing, where liquid is added to skimmed pan juices and boiled to reduce.

Resting a Roast Before Carving
Once a roast is removed from the oven or pot, it should be left in a warm place to "rest" 10–15 minutes. During this time, the temperature of the roast evens out, and the flesh reabsorbs most of the juices. Thus, the juices won't leak during carving.

1 ▲ Spoon off most of the fat from the roasting pan. Set the pan over medium-high heat on top of the stove. When the roasting juices begin to sizzle, whisk or stir in flour.

2 ▲ Cook, scraping the pan well to mix in all the browned bits from the bottom, until the mixture forms a smooth, brown paste. Add stock or another liquid, as specified in the recipe, and bring to a boil, stirring or whisking constantly. Simmer until the gravy has the right consistency, then season with salt and pepper.

Prime Rib of Beef with Shallots

SERVES 8

1 beef prime rib roast (4 ribs), weighing about 10 pounds, chined

vegetable oil

salt and pepper

1 pound plump shallots, unpeeled

1½ tablespoons flour

1½ cups beef stock, or 1 cup beef stock and ½ cup red wine

1 Preheat the oven to 350°F.

2 If the ends of the rib bones have been left on the roast you can scrape them clean, if desired. Rub any exposed bone ends with oil. Season the beef with salt and pepper. Set the beef in a roasting pan, fat side up.

3 Roast the beef until cooked to the desired degree of doneness, about 2 hours, basting often with the juices in the pan.

4 ▲ Meanwhile, peel off the outer, papery layers of skin from the shallots, leaving at least 2 layers. Trim the root and stem ends, if necessary.

5 About 30 minutes before the beef has finished cooking, put the shallots into the roasting pan around the beef.

6 When the beef is ready, transfer it to a carving board and set aside to rest at least 15 minutes. Remove the shallots from the pan and keep warm.

7 ▼ Spoon off all but 2 tablespoons of fat from the roasting pan. Mix in the flour, then add the stock and boil, stirring, until thickened.

8 Carve the beef. Serve with the gravy, the shallots still in their skins (they slip out easily), and roasted potatoes, if desired.

STEWING WITH A FRY-START

Fry-start stews have a wonderful rich flavor, due greatly to the initial searing – or browning – of the meat and vegetables. The long cooking period, in a seasoned liquid, produces a very tender and flavorful result. Be sure to use a heavy-based pan or casserole, such as a Dutch oven.

Saving the Flavor

If a different pan is used for searing the meat and vegetables, deglaze it: Add wine, stock, or water and bring to a boil, scraping up the browned bits from the bottom of the pan. Then add the resulting liquid to the stewpot.

1 ▲ Cut the meat into equal-sized cubes and dry it thoroughly with paper towels. Coat lightly with flour if the recipe directs.

2 ▲ Heat a little oil in a frying pan or flameproof casserole until it is very hot. Add a few cubes of meat – just enough to cover the bottom of the pan without touching each other. Do not crowd the meat in the pan. If the temperature drops too much, a crisp brown crust will not form.

3 ▲ Fry over medium-high heat until well browned on all sides. Turn the cubes so they brown evenly, and remove them as they are done.

4 ▲ Add the vegetables and cook, stirring occasionally, until they are well browned. Discard excess oil if directed in the recipe.

5 ▲ Return the meat to the pan. If flour is added now, sprinkle it over the meat and vegetables and let it brown, stirring well.

6 ▲ Add liquid barely to cover and stir to mix. Add any flavorings. Bring the liquid to a boil, then reduce the heat to a gentle simmer and complete the cooking as directed.

7 ▲ If flour hasn't been used already, the liquid may be thickened at the end of cooking. One method is butter and flour paste (1 tablespoon each per cup of liquid), stirred in gradually.

8 ▲ Or thicken with cornstarch (2 teaspoons diluted with 1 tablespoon water per cup of liquid); boil for 2–3 minutes, stirring. Or, simply boil the liquid to reduce it.

Beef Stew with Dumplings

SERVES 4

¼ cup flour
salt and pepper
1½ pounds boneless beef for stew, such as chuck or round, cut into 1½-inch cubes
3 tablespoons vegetable oil
2 large onions, chopped
2 celery stalks, coarsely chopped
2 large carrots, thickly sliced
2 turnips, cut into cubes
1½ cups cubed rutabaga
2 cups beef stock
1 tablespoon soy sauce
1 bay leaf
1½ teaspoons fresh thyme leaves, or ½ teaspoon dried thyme
FOR THE DUMPLINGS
1 cup flour
2 teaspoons baking powder
½ teaspoon salt
¼ teaspoon English mustard powder
⅔ cup milk
2 tablespoons vegetable oil

1 Put the flour in a plastic bag and season. Add the beef cubes, a few at a time, and toss to coat. Remove them, shaking off excess flour.

2 ▲ Heat the oil in a Dutch oven or other flameproof casserole over medium-high heat. Add the cubes of beef, in batches, and brown them well on all sides. Remove them from the casserole as they are browned.

3 Add the onions, celery, carrots, turnips, and rutabaga. Brown them all over, stirring frequently.

4 ▲ Return the beef cubes to the casserole. Add the stock, soy sauce, bay leaf, and thyme. Bring to a boil, stirring well to mix in the browned bits from the bottom of the pan.

5 Cover tightly, then reduce the heat to very low. Simmer until the beef is very tender, about 2 hours.

6 For the dumplings, sift the dry ingredients into a bowl. Add the milk and oil and stir just until the dry ingredients are bound into a soft, batter-like dough.

7 ▲ Uncover the casserole and bring the stew liquid back to a boil. Drop the dumpling dough onto the surface of the stew, in 8–10 dollops.

8 Cover again and simmer over low heat until the dumplings are just set and fluffy, 12–15 minutes. Serve hot, directly from the casserole.

~ **VARIATION** ~

For Beef Pot Pie, omit dumplings and put the stew in a baking dish. Cover with pie pastry and bake at 400°F for 25 minutes.

SEARING MEAT FOR POT-ROASTING OR ROASTING

Large cuts and pieces of meat to be roasted or pot-roasted are sometimes seared as the initial step in cooking. This may be done either by roasting briefly at a high temperature and then reducing the heat, or by frying. The result is a browned crust that adds delicious flavor.

Pot-Roasting or Braising

This method of cooking tenderizes even the thoughest cuts of meat. Prime cuts can also be pot-roasted, but cooking times are cut short – just long enough to reach the degree of doneness you like. Depending on the desired result, meat to be pot-roasted or braised may or may not have an initial searing.

1 ▲ To sear by frying: Dry the meat well with paper towels. Heat a little oil in a frying pan, flameproof casserole, or roasting pan until it is very hot. Put in the meat and fry over high heat until it is well browned on all surfaces. Turn the meat using two spatulas or spoons. (Piercing with a fork would let juices escape, which would be boiled away.)

2 ▲ If roasting, transfer the meat, in its roasting pan, to the oven. If pot-roasting, add a small amount of liquid and cover the pot tightly. If a frying pan has been used for searing, be sure to deglaze it: add some of the liquid called for in the recipe and bring to a boil, scraping up the browned bits from the bottom. Add this flavorful mixture to the pot.

Veal Pot Roast with Herbs

SERVES 6

1 tablespoon vegetable oil

3-pound boned veal shoulder roast, rolled and tied

4 medium onions, quartered

½ cup chicken stock or water

a few sprigs each of fresh thyme, marjoram, and rosemary, or ¾ teaspoon each dried thyme, oregano, and rosemary

salt and pepper

1 Preheat the oven to 300°F.

2 Heat the oil in a Dutch oven or other flameproof casserole over high heat (choose a casserole not much larger than the veal roast). Put in the veal roast and brown it, turning frequently to color it evenly on all sides.

3 ▼ Add the onions, stock, and herbs. Season with salt and pepper. Cover and transfer to the oven. Cook until well done, 2½–3 hours.

Other Cuts for Pot-Roasting

Other large roasts can be pot-roasted in the same way as the veal. For instance, use pork shoulder arm or butt roasts.

4 ▲ Transfer the veal roast to a carving board. Remove the onions and keep warm. Let the veal rest at least 10 minutes. Discard the strings before carving.

5 Skim the cooking juices to remove all fat. Bring to a boil, then strain. Taste for seasoning. Serve with the veal and onions.

PAN-FRYING AND SAUTÉING

Tender cuts of meat, such as steaks and chops, slices of calf's liver, and hamburgers are ideal for cooking quickly in a heavy frying pan. And the juices left in the pan can be turned into an easy sauce.

Before pan-frying and sautéing, trim excess fat from steaks, chops, scaloppine, etc., then dry thoroughly with paper towels.

For cooking, use a fat that can be heated to a high temperature. If using butter, adding an equal amount of vegetable oil will help prevent burning, or use clarified butter.

1 ▲ Heat the fat in the pan over high heat until very hot but not browning. Put in the meat, in one layer, without crowding.

2 ▲ Fry until browned on both sides and done to your taste. If pan-frying pork or veal chops, reduce the heat to medium once they are in the pan.

Testing Steak for Doneness
A reliable way to test steak is by pressing it with your finger. When raw, it is soft and can be squashed. When cooked rare, it will be only slightly springy. When cooked medium, it will offer more resistance and drops of red juice will appear on the surface. When well done, it will be firm to the touch.

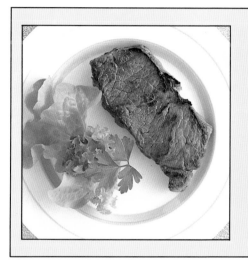

Pan-Fried Teriyaki Steak
Combine 3 tablespoons vegetable oil, 1 tablespoon each soy sauce, honey, red wine vinegar, and minced onion, 1 minced garlic clove, and ½ teaspoon ground ginger in a heavy-duty plastic bag. Add 4 boneless sirloin steaks and turn so they are well coated. Let marinate 2 hours. Drain the steaks and pat dry, then pan-fry to the desired degree of doneness. The steaks can also be broiled or grilled. *Serves 4.*

DEGLAZING FOR A PAN SAUCE

After pan-frying or sautéing, a simple yet delicious sauce can be made in the pan. The same method can be used to make gravy for roasted meat. Deglazing is also a good way to maximize flavor when making stews and casseroles.

Before deglazing, remove the meat and keep it warm. Pour or spoon off all the fat from the pan, unless the recipe calls for shallots, garlic, etc. to be softened. In that case, leave 1–2 teaspoons of fat and cook the vegetables in it.

1 ▲ Pour in the liquid called for in the recipe (wine, stock, vinegar, etc.). Bring to a boil, stirring well to scrape up all the browned bits from the bottom of the pan and dissolve them in the liquid.

2 ▲ Boil over high heat until the liquid is almost syrupy. (The time needed to reduce the liquid depends on the amount used.) If the recipe directs, enrich the sauce with cream or butter. Season with salt and pepper and serve.

STIR-FRYING

The preparation of ingredients for stir-frying often takes longer than the cooking itself. This is because all ingredients must be cut to uniform sizes so that the cooking can be accomplished quickly and evenly.

A wok is excellent for stir-frying because its high sides let you stir and toss the ingredients briskly. Use long cooking chopsticks or a wooden spatula to keep the ingredients moving around the wok.

Stir-Fried Beef with Snow Peas
Cut 1 pound lean, boneless, tender beef into very thin strips. Combine 3 tablespoons soy sauce, 2 tablespoons dry sherry, 1 tablespoon brown sugar, and ½ teaspoon cornstarch in a bowl. Heat 1 tablespoon vegetable oil in the hot wok. Add 1 tablespoon each minced fresh ginger and minced garlic and stir-fry 30 seconds. Add the beef and stir-fry until well browned, about 2 minutes. Add ½ pound snow peas and stir-fry 3 minutes longer. Stir the soy sauce mixture until smooth, then add to the wok. Bring to a boil, stirring and tossing, and simmer the mixture until just thickened and smooth. Serve immediately, accompanied by freshly cooked rice. *Serves 4.*

1 ▲ Prepare all the ingredients following recipe directions.

3 ▲ When the oil is hot (a piece of vegetable should sizzle on contact), add the ingredients in the order directed in the recipe. (Those that take longer to cook are added first.) Do not add too much to the wok at a time or the ingredients will start to steam rather than fry.

2 ▲ Heat a wok or large, deep skillet over medium-high heat. Dribble in the oil down the sides.

4 ▲ Fry, stirring and tossing constantly with chopsticks or a spatula, until the ingredients are just cooked: vegetables should be crisp-tender and meat and poultry tender and juicy.

5 ◄ Push the ingredients to the side of the wok, or remove them. Pour liquid or sauce, as specified in the recipe, into the bottom. Cook and stir, then mix in the ingredients from the sides. Serve immediately.

MAKING MEAT STOCK

The most delicious meat soups, stews, casseroles, gravies, and sauces rely on a good homemade stock for success. Neither a bouillon cube nor a canned bouillon or broth will do if you want the best flavor. Once made, meat stock can be kept in the refrigerator 4–5 days, or frozen for longer storage (up to 6 months).

On the Light Side
For a light meat stock, use veal bones and do not roast the bones or vegetables. Put in the pot with cold water and cook as described.

MAKES ABOUT 2 QUARTS

4 pounds beef, veal, or lamb bones, such as shank, knuckle, leg, and neck, cut into 2½-inch pieces
2 onions, unpeeled, quartered
2 carrots, roughly chopped
2 celery stalks, with leaves if possible, roughly chopped
2 tomatoes, coarsely chopped
4½ quarts cold water
a handful of parsley stems
a few fresh thyme sprigs, or ¾ teaspoon dried thyme
2 bay leaves
10 black peppercorns, lightly crushed

1 ▲ Preheat the oven to 450°F. Put the bones in a roasting pan or flameproof casserole and roast, turning occasionally, until they start to brown, about 30 minutes.

2 ▲ Add the onions, carrots, celery, and tomatoes and baste with the fat in the pan. Roast until the bones are browned, about 30 minutes longer. Stir and baste from time to time.

3 ▲ Transfer the bones and vegetables to a stockpot. Spoon off the fat from the roasting pan.

4 ▲ Add a little of the water to the roasting pan and bring to a boil on top of the stove, stirring well to scrape up any browned bits. Pour this liquid into the stockpot.

5 ▲ Add the remaining water. Bring just to a boil, skimming frequently to remove all the foam from the surface. Add the herbs and peppercorns.

6 ▲ Partly cover the pot and simmer the stock 4–6 hours. The bones and vegetables should always be covered with liquid, so add a little boiling water from time to time if necessary.

7 ▲ Strain the stock through a strainer. Skim as much fat as possible from the surface. To remove all the fat, let the stock cool, then refrigerate it; the fat will rise to the top and set in a layer that can be removed easily.

FISH & SEAFOOD

~

Fish and seafood are simple to cook and excellent for a quick meal. The techniques show ways to cook fish by baking, broiling, poaching and frying methods, how to make fish stock, and how to prepare live shellfish.

PREPARING WHOLE FISH FOR COOKING

Most fish have scales and these should be removed before cooking unless the fish is to be filleted or the skin is to be removed before serving. Fish sold in markets is normally scaled as well as cleaned (eviscerated or drawn), but you can do this yourself, if necessary. Trimming the tail gives a whole fish a neat appearance.

All fish preparation is best done in or near the sink, with cool water running. Salt your hands for a good grip on fish.

1 ▲ To scale: Grasp the tail firmly and scrape off the scales using a special fish scaler or a knife, working from the tail toward the head. Rinse the fish well. Repeat on the other side.

2 ▲ To trim: For flatfish to be cooked whole, use kitchen scissors to trim off the outer half of the small fin bones all around the fish.

3 ▲ For round fish, cut the flesh on both sides of the anal and dorsal (back) fins and pull them out; the small bones attached will come out, too. Trim off the other fins.

4 ▲ If the fish is to be cooked whole, leave the fins on, or just trim them, because they help keep the shape of the fish.

5 ▲ To trim the tail: If the tail is to be left on, cut a neat "V" in the center with scissors. The fish is now dressed for cooking.

A LOOK AT FISH

In terms of shape and structure, most fish fall into one of two general categories: round fish and flatfish.

Round fish have thicker bodies and many of their bones are attached to their fins. They can be filleted or cut into steaks, but both will contain small pin bones.

Flatfish have a flat central bone with a row of bones attached on either side. This simple bone structure makes flatfish easy to fillet. Most are too thin to cut into steaks.

Large fish such as tuna have a thick bone running down the center of their bodies; spiking out from this are four rows of bones that divide the flesh into quarters. These boneless "loins" are usually cut into slices called steaks.

The fat content of fish is an important consideration in deciding how to cook it. Lean fish can dry out at high temperatures, so a protective coating is a good idea when frying. When broiling, marinate or baste them. Lean and moderately lean fish are best cooked by moist methods such as steaming, poaching, or baking in a sauce. Oily fish, however, almost baste themselves during cooking, so

they are ideal for broiling, grilling, and pan-frying.

Texture and flavor are also important to consider in choosing how to prepare fish. If the flavor of the flesh is mild, it is important not to overwhelm it. But fish with rich, distinctively flavored flesh will stand up well to spicy, pungent seasonings.

Fish that are delicate in texture need careful cooking. Pan-frying with a flour coating, steaming, and gentle baking are best. However, fish with meaty, dense flesh can be cubed and put onto skewers.

Pan-Fried Trout with Olives and Capers

SERVES 4

4 whole trout, ¾–1 pound each, cleaned and trimmed
salt and pepper
flour, for coating
¼ cup vegetable oil
6–8 tablespoons butter
½ cup sliced black olives
3 tablespoons capers
2 tablespoons lemon juice
lemon wedges, for serving

1 ▲ Sprinkle the trout with salt and pepper. Coat them lightly with flour, shaking off any excess.

Terms Used in the Fish Market
Drawn: Whole fish that has had its internal organs removed. Other terms used are cleaned, gutted, and eviscerated. The gills may also have been removed.
Dressed: Whole fish that has been drawn and scaled. Another term for this is whole-dressed.
Pan-dressed: Whole fish that has been drawn and scaled and the head, tail, and fins removed.
Fillet: Boneless piece cut lengthwise from the sides of the fish. May or may not be skinned.
Steak: Slice cut crosswise from a whole dressed fish.

2 ▲ Heat the oil in a large frying pan over medium heat. Add the trout and fry until golden brown on both sides and cooked through, 12–15 minutes.

3 Transfer the trout to a warmed serving platter and keep warm. Pour off all the oil from the pan.

4 ▼ Add the butter to the frying pan and melt it. When it starts to brown and smell nutty, stir in the olives, capers, and lemon juice. Cook 10 seconds, then pour this sauce over the fish. Serve immediately.

BAKING FISH

Most fish are suitable for baking – whole or in fillets or steaks. Lean fish, in particular, benefit from some protection so they don't dry out, such as a stuffing or coating, or baking them in a little liquid or sauce, which can also be served with the fish. All of these add extra flavor to the fish, too.

Cooking in foil or paper is suitable for many fish, both whole ones and fillets and steaks. This method seals in moisture, so is similar in effect to steaming. It's a good solution for fish too large to fit in a steamer or poacher.

A good rule of thumb for cooking time is 10 minutes in a hot oven (425°F) to each inch, calculated at the thickest part of the fish.

1 ▲ To bake fish with liquid: Pour over a small amount of stock, wine, water, or other liquid as directed, and add flavorings and seasonings.

2 ▲ To bake fish in foil or paper: Wrap tightly with seasonings and flavorings as directed and place the package on a baking sheet.

Baked Fish Steaks
Arrange 1½ pounds white fish steaks in a shallow baking dish. Sprinkle the fish with 2 tablespoons minced shallot or onion and 3 tablespoons lemon juice or dry white wine. Drizzle with 2 tablespoons melted butter and season with salt and pepper to taste. Bake in a preheated 425°F oven until the fish is done, about 10 minutes. Pour the cooking juices over the steaks before serving. *Serves 4.*

A SELECTION OF FISH VARIETIES

Choose the freshest fish you can find. If necessary, substitute another variety with similar qualities.

Lean Fish
Cod (Scrod, if young)
- round fish, saltwater
- flaky, tender texture; mild flavor
- broil, bake, steam, poach
- substitute haddock, halibut, lingcod

Flounder
- flatfish, saltwater
- fine texture; delicate flavor
- fry, broil, bake, steam
- substitute sole, whitefish, orange roughy

Grouper
- round fish, saltwater
- firm, medium-dense texture; mild flavor
- bake, fry
- substitute cod, monkfish, sea bass

Haddock
- round fish, saltwater
- soft, moist texture; mild flavor
- broil, bake, steam, poach
- substitute cod, halibut

Halibut
- flatfish, saltwater
- firm, moist texture; mild, sweet
- broil, bake, steam, poach
- substitute flounder, sole

Mahimahi (Dolphinfish)
- thick central bone, saltwater
- firm, medium-dense; mild, sweet
- bake, broil, fry
- substitute grouper, halibut

Perch
- round fish, freshwater
- firm, flaky texture; mild flavor
- fry, broil, bake
- substitute trout, Atlantic perch, catfish

Red snapper
- round fish, saltwater
- firm, moist texture; mild, sweet
- bake, broil, steam, poach
- substitute trout, whitefish

Rockfish (Striped bass)
- round fish, saltwater (spawns in freshwater)
- tender texture; slightly sweet
- bake, poach, fry
- substitute trout, grouper

TESTING FOR DONENESS

All seafood cooks quickly. If overcooked, it becomes dry and loses its succulent quality. In the case of meaty fish such as tuna and swordfish, it can be unpleasantly chewy. It is therefore worth knowing how to judge when fish is perfectly cooked.

The flesh of raw fish and crustaceans is translucent; it becomes opaque when it is cooked. However, as fish will continue cooking from residual heat, it should be removed from the heat source before it is entirely opaque.

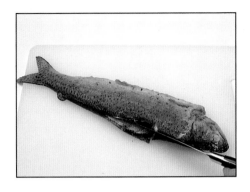

1 ▲ To determine whether a fish is cooked, make a small slit in the thickest part. Lift with the knife to look into the opening.

2 ▲ The fish is ready when still very slightly translucent in the center or near the bone, but the rest of the flesh is opaque throughout.

Sea bass
- round fish, saltwater
- flaky or firm flesh; mild flavor
- broil, fry, bake
- substitute salmon

Sole
- flatfish, saltwater
- fine texture; delicate flavor
- fry, broil, bake, poach
- substitute flounder

Moderately Lean Fish
Catfish
- round fish, freshwater
- soft, moist texture; mild, sweet
- fry, steam, poach
- substitute trout

Orange roughy
- round fish, saltwater
- firm, moist texture; delicate, sweet flavor
- bake, steam, poach
- substitute cod

Porgy (Scup, Sea bream)
- round fish, saltwater
- firm, moist texture; mild, sweet
- fry, broil, bake, steam
- substitute perch, butterfish

Sea trout (Weakfish)
- round fish, saltwater
- moist, flaky texture; mild, sweet
- broil, bake, fry
- substitute cod, haddock, bluefish

Swordfish
- thick central bone, saltwater
- firm, meaty texture; mild
- broil, bake, steam, poach
- substitute shark, tuna

Trout
- round fish, freshwater
- tender, flaky texture; mild, rich
- fry, broil, bake
- substitute salmon, whitefish

Tuna
- thick central bone, saltwater
- meaty texture; mild to strong
- bake, steam, poach, broil
- substitute salmon, swordfish

Moderately Oily and Oily Fish
Bluefish
- round fish, saltwater
- fine, moist texture; mild flavor if small, more distinctive in larger fish
- bake, broil, fry
- substitute flounder, lake trout

Carp
- round fish, freshwater
- soft, flaky texture; mild flavor
- bake, broil, fry, steam
- substitute cod, haddock

Mackerel
- round fish, saltwater
- moist and tender or firm texture; rich, distinctive flavor
- broil, bake, steam, poach
- substitute tuna

Pompano
- round fish, saltwater
- firm, moist texture; sweet flavor
- broil, bake, fry
- substitute sole, bluefish, red snapper

Salmon
- round fish, freshwater/saltwater
- flaky, tender texture; mild to rich
- bake, broil, steam, poach
- substitute swordfish, tuna, trout

Whitefish
- round fish, freshwater
- tender, flaky texture; mild, sweet
- bake, broil, fry
- substitute haddock, lake trout

POACHING FISH

Whole fish, large and small, as well as fillets and steaks are excellent poached because the gentle cooking gives succulent results. Poached fish can be served hot or cold, with a wide variety of sauces. The poaching liquid may be used as the basis for a sauce.

Poaching Containers
A long rectangular fish poacher with a perforated rack enables you to lift the fish out of the liquid after cooking. You could also use a rack set in a deep roasting pan such as that for turkey.

1 ▲ To oven-poach small whole fish, fillets, or steaks: Place the fish in a buttered, flameproof dish that is large enough to hold the pieces comfortably. Pour in enough liquid to come two-thirds of the way up the side of the fish.

2 ▲ Add any flavorings called for in the recipe. Press a piece of buttered wax paper on top to keep in the moisture without sticking to the fish.

3 ▲ Set the dish over medium heat and bring the liquid just to a boil. Transfer the dish to a preheated 350°F oven and poach until the fish is just cooked. To test, with the tip of a sharp knife, make a small cut into the thickest part of the fish (ideally next to a bone): the flesh should be very slightly translucent in the center.

4 ▲ To poach whole fish, fillets, or steaks on the top of the stove: Put large whole fish on the rack in a fish poacher, or set it on a piece of cheesecloth that can be used like a hammock. Put small whole fish, fillets, and steaks on a rack, or set directly in a baking dish, wide saucepan, or frying pan.

5 ▲ Prepare the poaching liquid (salted water, milk, wine, stock, or court bouillon) in the fish poacher or in a large roasting pan (or a wide saucepan or frying pan for fillets and steaks). Set the rack in the poacher, or the cheesecloth hammock in the roasting pan. Add more liquid, if necessary, to cover the fish.

6 ▲ Cover the poacher or pan and bring the liquid just to a boil. Reduce the heat and simmer very gently until the fish is cooked.

Poached Sole Fillets
Oven-poach 8 skinless sole fillets, each ½-inch thick (about 1½ pounds). Use 1 cup dry white wine or fish stock, to almost cover, with ¼ cup minced scallions, 4–6 lemon slices, and a few allspice berries for flavoring. Simmer 3–5 minutes, then remove the fish. Boil the cooking liquid until reduced to about ¼ cup, then strain it. Season with salt and pepper. *Serves 4.*

STEAMING FISH

This simple, moist-heat method of cooking is ideal for fish and shellfish. If you don't have a steamer, it is easy to improvise.

Steamed Salmon with Herbs
Line a heatproof plate with fresh herb sprigs (dill, parsley, chives, etc.). Set 2 portions of seasoned salmon fillet, each 1-inch thick, on top. Steam Chinese-style about 10 minutes. If desired, top with flavored butter or serve with a sauce such as Hollandaise. *Serves 2.*

1 ▲ Using a steamer: Arrange the fish on the rack in the steamer and set over boiling water. Cover and steam until done.

3 ▲ Steaming larger fish and fillets: Arrange the fish on a rack in a roasting pan of boiling water or on a plate set on the rack. Cover tightly with foil and steam until done.

2 ▲ Chinese-style steaming: Arrange the fish on a heatproof plate that will fit inside a bamboo steamer or wok. Put the plate on the rack in a steamer or wok; set over boiling water. Cover and steam until done.

4 ▲ Steaming in foil: Wrap the fish and seasonings in foil, sealing well, and set on a rack in the steamer or in a large roasting pan of boiling water. Steam until done.

CUTTING FISH STEAKS

Round fish, such as cod or salmon, and large flatfish, such as halibut or turbot, are often cut into steaks for cooking. The usual range of thickness for the steaks is 1–1½ inches. Steaks cut from the tail are smaller, but may contain fewer bones.

1 ▲ With a large, sharp knife, slice the fish crosswise, perpendicular to the backbone, into steaks of the desired thickness.

2 ▲ If necessary, cut through the backbone with kitchen scissors or a knife with a serrated blade.

CUTTING FISH FILLETS

Fillets are boneless pieces of fish, and for this reason are very popular. A sharp filleting knife, with its thin, flexible blade, is the tool to use for removing the fillets. Be sure to keep all the bones and trimmings for making stock.

Round fish are easy to fillet and they produce a boneless piece from each side. Large flatfish are also easy to deal with, although they are filleted slightly differently from round fish and yield 4 narrow fillets – 2 from each side.

Filleting Small Flatfish
You can take 2 fillets from smaller flatfish (one from each side). Cut behind the head and down the sides of the fish as above, but do not make the central cut. Starting from the head end on one side and working down the fish, cut the flesh away from the rib bones until you reach the center (the backbone). Rotate the fish and repeat on the other side to cut away the whole fillet. Turn the fish over and repeat to cut away the second whole fillet.

---

1 ▲ To fillet a round fish: First cut off the head. With the tip of the knife, cut through the skin all along the length of the backbone.

3 ▲ When you reach the tail, cut across to release the fillet. Repeat the procedure on the other side to remove the other fillet.

2 ▲ Working from head to tail and holding the knife almost parallel to the fish, use short strokes to cut 1 fillet off the rib bones in one piece. Follow the slit cut along the backbone.

4 ▲ Run your fingers over the flesh side of each fillet to locate any stray bones. Pull them out with tweezers.

5 ▲ To fillet a flatfish: Lay the fish on the work surface and make a curved cut behind the head, cutting down to but not through the backbone. With the tip of the knife, slit the skin down both sides of the fish where the fin bones meet the rib bones, "outlining" the fillets, and slit across the tail.

6 ▲ Slit straight down the center line of the fish, from head to tail, cutting down to the backbone. Working from the center at the head end, cut 1 fillet neatly away from the rib bones on one side. Hold the knife blade almost parallel to the fish and use short strokes.

7 ▲ Rotate the fish and cut away the second fillet. Turn the fish over and repeat to remove the 2 fillets on the other side. Pull out any stray bones with tweezers.

BROILING FISH

The intense dry heat of this method of cooking is best used for fish with a lot of natural oil, such as salmon, mackerel, and tuna. However, leaner fish can also be broiled, as long as you baste them frequently to keep them moist or cook them in a little liquid.

Always preheat the broiler. If desired, line the broiler pan with foil to save on clean up.

Fish can also be very successfully grilled over charcoal. Choose full-flavored fish that will not be overwhelmed by the smoky taste. Thin pieces are easier to handle if placed in a hinged wire fish basket. Be sure to baste well during cooking to prevent the fish from drying out.

Fish Kabobs with Lemon Butter
Combine 2 tablespoons each melted butter and lemon juice with 1 teaspoon English mustard powder and 1 minced garlic clove. Cut 1½ pounds halibut, grouper, or sea bass steaks into 1-inch cubes. Thread onto skewers with pieces of red bell pepper. Brush with the butter mixture and broil, basting frequently and turning to cook evenly, until done. *Serves 4.*

1 ▲ To broil oilier fish (small whole fish, boned and butterflied fish, fillets and steaks that are at least ½-inch thick, or cubes of fish on skewers): Rinse the fish and pat it dry with paper towels. Marinate the fish if the recipe directs.

3 ▲ Set the fish under the broiler, 3–4 inches from the heat (thin pieces should be closer to the heat than thicker ones). Broil, basting once or twice and turning if the recipe directs, until the fish is done.

2 ▲ Preheat the broiler with the broiler pan in place. When hot, lightly brush the hot pan with oil or line with foil and then brush with oil. Arrange the fish in the pan, in one layer, skin-side down. Brush the fish with butter, oil, or a basting mixture, according to the recipe directions.

4 ▲ To broil leaner fish (small whole fish, and fish steaks and fillets that are at least ½-inch thick and prepared for cooking as above): Arrange in a buttered flameproof dish. Add a little liquid (wine, stock, etc.) just to cover the bottom of the dish. Brush the fish with butter, oil, or a basting mixture, according to the recipe directions. Broil the fish as above, without turning.

BREADING AND FRYING FISH

Fish to be fried is often coated with crumbs, or with a batter. The coating keeps the fish moist and full of flavor as well as making a crisp or crunchy crust. Many other foods – boneless chicken breast halves, veal scaloppine, and vegetables, for example – are also breaded.

1 ▲ Lightly beat egg in a shallow dish. Spread flour on a plate or sheet of wax paper. Season it with salt and pepper (or as recipe directs). Spread crumbs (fine bread crumbs, crushed crackers, cornmeal, etc.) on another.

2 ▲ To bread large pieces of fish: Dip first in the flour, turning to coat both sides lightly and evenly. Shake or brush off the excess flour.

Deep-Fried Catfish
Bread 8 catfish fillets, using seasoned flour, egg, and cornmeal. Pan-fry or deep-fry and serve with lemon wedges. *Serves 4.*

3 ▲ Next, dip the floured fish in the egg, turning to moisten both sides.

4 ▲ Dredge the fish in the crumbs, turning to coat evenly. Press to help the crumbs adhere. Shake or pat off excess crumbs. Refrigerate to set the coating, at least 20 minutes.

5 ▲ To bread small pieces of fish (strips of fish fillet, shrimp, etc.): Put the crumbs in a plastic bag. After dipping the fish in flour and egg, toss a few pieces at a time in the bag of crumbs to coat them.

6 ▲ To pan-fry: Heat oil or a mixture of oil and butter in a frying pan (enough fat to coat the bottom of the pan in a thin layer). When it is very hot, put the fish in the pan, in one layer. Fry until golden brown on both sides and the fish is done. Drain on paper towels before serving.

7 ▲ To deep-fry: Half fill a deep pan with oil and heat it to 375°F on a deep-frying thermometer. Gently lower the breaded pieces of fish into the hot oil (frying them only a few at a time). Fry until golden brown, turning them occasionally so that they cook evenly. Remove and drain on paper towels before serving.

PREPARING CLAMS AND MUSSELS

Mollusks such as clams and mussels should be eaten very fresh and must be alive when you buy them and cook them (unless they have been shucked and frozen). They are alive if their shells are tightly closed; any shells that are open should close promptly when tapped. Dead clams or mussels, or any with broken shells, should be discarded.

If you have dug the clams yourself, let them stand in a bucket of sea water for several hours, changing the water once or twice. (Do not use fresh water because it will kill the clams.) Add a handful or two of cornmeal to the water to help clean the clams' stomachs. Clams bought in the fish market will have been purged of sand.

1 ▲ Scrub the shells of mussels with a stiff brush and rinse well. Scrub clams under cool running water.

2 ▲ Before cooking mussels, pull off their "beards" (their anchor threads) with the help of a small knife. Rinse the mussels well.

3 ▲ **To steam:** Put a little dry white wine or water in a large pot, with flavorings as the recipe directs. Add the clams or mussels, cover tightly, and bring to a boil. Steam until the shells open, 5–10 minutes, shaking the pot occasionally.

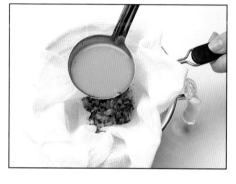

4 ▲ Serve the clams or mussels in their shells, or shuck them before using. Strain the cooking liquid (which will include all the delicious liquor from the shells) and spoon it over the clams or mussels, or use it as the basis for a sauce.

Sailor's Mussels
Prepare 2–3 quarts live mussels. Steam with 1 cup dry white wine or fish or chicken stock, 1 small onion, chopped, 1–2 minced garlic cloves, and ½ cup minced fresh parsley. With a slotted spoon, transfer the opened mussels to large bowls. Add 3 tablespoons butter to the cooking liquid and stir until melted, then add pepper. Pour this liquid over the mussels. *Serves 4.*

5 ▲ **To shuck a live clam or mussel:** Hold it firmly in one hand, with the hinge in your palm. Insert the side of a clam or oyster knife blade between the shell halves and work it around to cut through the hinge muscle.

6 ▲ Open the shell and cut the clam or mussel free of the shell. Do this over a bowl in order to catch all the liquor from the shell. (Clams are sometimes eaten raw, but mussels are always cooked.)

PEELING AND DEVEINING SHRIMP

Shrimp can be cooked in their shells, but more often they are peeled first (the shells can be used to make an aromatic stock). The intestinal vein that runs down the back of the shrimp is removed mainly because of its appearance, although if the shrimp are large, the vein may contain grit. The deveining slit may be cut further to open out, or butterfly, the shrimp.

Shrimp are occasionally sold with their heads. These are easily pulled off, and will enhance the flavor of stock made with the shells.

1 ▲ Holding the shrimp firmly in one hand, pull off the legs with the fingers of the other hand.

2 ▲ Peel the shell away from the body. When you reach the tail, hold the body and pull away the tail; the shell will come off with it. Or, you can leave the tail on the shrimp and just remove the body shell.

3 ▲ Make a shallow cut down the center of the curved back of the shrimp. Pull out the black vein with a toothpick or your fingers.

4 ▲ **To butterfly shrimp**: Cut along the deveining slit to split open the shrimp, without cutting all the way through. Open up the shrimp flat.

5 ▲ **To devein shrimp in the shell**: Insert a toothpick crosswise in several places along the back where the shell overlaps to lift out the vein.

Spicy Butterflied Shrimp

SERVES 4–6

6 tablespoons olive oil
1/3 cup orange juice
1/4 cup lime juice
1 large garlic clove, minced
1 teaspoon allspice berries, crushed
1/4 teaspoon hot pepper flakes
salt and pepper
2 pounds raw large or jumbo shrimp, peeled, deveined, and butterflied
lime wedges, for serving

1 ▲ Combine the oil, fruit juices, garlic, allspice, pepper flakes, and seasoning in a large shallow baking dish. Add the shrimp and turn to coat completely with the spiced oil.

2 Cover the dish and let the shrimp marinate for 1 hour at room temperature or for at least 2 hours in the refrigerator.

3 Preheat the broiler.

4 Spread out the shrimp in one layer in the baking dish, arranging them cut side up as much as possible. Broil about 4 inches from the heat until the flesh becomes opaque, 6-8 minutes. There is no need to turn the shrimp.

5 Serve hot, with lime wedges.

Scallops Wrapped in Prosciutto

SERVES 4

24 medium sea scallops, prepared for cooking

lemon juice

8–12 slices of prosciutto, cut lengthwise into 2 or 3 strips

olive oil

pepper

lemon wedges, for serving

1 Preheat the broiler or prepare a charcoal fire.

2 Sprinkle the scallops with lemon juice. Wrap a strip of prosciutto around each scallop. Thread onto 8 skewers.

3 ▲ Brush with oil. Arrange on a baking sheet if broiling. Broil about 4 inches from the heat, or grill over charcoal, until the scallops are opaque, 4-5 minutes on each side.

4 Set 2 skewers on each plate. Sprinkle the scallops with freshly ground black pepper and serve with lemon wedges, if desired.

Preparing Scallops
Scallops are usually shucked at sea, and the shell and coral-colored roe are discarded. Only large sea scallops need further preparation.

Pull off and discard the small piece of gristle from the side of the scallop. Rinse the scallop well to remove any grit, and pat dry.

Spicy Butterflied Shrimp (left), Scallops Wrapped in Prosciutto

MAKING FISH STOCK

Fish stock is much quicker to make than meat or poultry stock. You may have the basic ingredients, or ask your fish merchant for heads and bones.

MAKES ABOUT 1 QUART

1½ pounds heads, bones, and trimmings from white fish (not strong, oily fish)

1 onion, sliced

2 celery stalks with leaves, chopped

1 carrot, sliced

½ lemon, sliced (optional)

1 bay leaf

a few fresh parsley sprigs

6 black peppercorns

5½ cups water

½ cup dry white wine

1 ▲ Rinse the fish heads, bones, and trimmings well under cold running water. Put in a stockpot with the vegetables, lemon, if using, the herbs, peppercorns, water, and wine. Bring to a boil, skimming the surface frequently, then reduce the heat and simmer 25 minutes.

2 ▲ Strain the stock without pressing down on the ingredients in the strainer. If not using immediately, let cool and then refrigerate. Fish stock should be used within 2 days, or it can be frozen up to 3 months.

Fisherman's Stew

SERVES 4

6 slices of bacon, cut into strips

1 tablespoon butter

1 large onion, chopped

1 garlic clove, minced

2 tablespoons chopped fresh parsley

1 teaspoon fresh thyme leaves or ½ teaspoon dried thyme

2 cups peeled, seeded, and chopped tomatoes, or canned crushed tomatoes

½ cup dry vermouth or dry white wine

2 cups fish stock

2 cups diced potatoes

1½–2 pounds skinless white fish fillets, cut into large chunks

salt and pepper

1 Fry the bacon in a large saucepan over medium heat until lightly browned but not crisp, then remove and drain on paper towels. Pour off all but about 1 tablespoon of fat.

2 ▲ Add the butter to the pan and cook the onion, stirring occasionally, until soft, about 3–5 minutes. Add the garlic and herbs and continue cooking for 1 minute, stirring. Add the tomatoes, vermouth or wine, and stock and bring to a boil.

3 Reduce the heat, cover, and simmer the stew for 15 minutes. Add the potatoes, cover again, and simmer until they are almost tender, about 10–12 minutes.

4 ▼ Add the chunks of fish and the bacon. Simmer gently, uncovered, until the fish is just cooked and the potatoes are tender, about 5 minutes longer. Taste for seasoning and serve.

~ COOK'S TIP ~

For fish stock, use heads, bones, and trimmings only from mild, white-fleshed fish, not from strong-flavored oily fish.

Pasta, Grains & Pulses

~

These staple foods are simple to cook and nutritious, offering a delicious alternative to meat. This chapter looks at ways of preparation and cooking techniques, and shows you how to make your own pasta.

COOKING PASTA

Both fresh and dried pasta are cooked in the same way. The golden rules for success are: use plenty of water and keep checking the pasta to be sure it does not overcook.

Fresh pasta will cook much more quickly than dried – in 1–4 minutes as opposed to 5 minutes or more.

Buttered Noodles

Cook 1 pound fettuccine or tagliatelle (fresh or dried) until "al dente." Drain well and return to the pot. Add 3–4 tablespoons butter and ⅛ teaspoon freshly grated nutmeg. Season with salt and pepper. Toss until the noodles are coated, then serve. *Serves 6*.

Buttered Noodles with Herbs

Omit the nutmeg and add ¼ cup minced fresh herbs such as parsley, dill, basil, or thyme – singly or a mixture.

Buttered Noodles with Cheese

Add 3 tablespoons freshly grated Parmesan cheese.

1 ▲ Bring a very large pot of salted water to a boil. (Use at least 4 quarts of water and 2 teaspoons salt to 1 pound of pasta.) Drop in the pasta all at once and stir to separate the shapes or strands.

3 ▲ Bring the water back to a boil, then reduce the heat slightly and boil until the pasta is just done. For dried pasta, follow the package directions, but start testing as soon as you reach the minimum time given. To test, lift a piece of pasta out on a wooden fork or slotted spoon. Cut it in half. There should be no sign of opaque, uncooked pasta in the center. Or bite it – it should be tender but still firm. In Italian, this is when it is "al dente," or to the tooth.

2 ▲ If you are cooking spaghetti, let the ends in the water soften slightly and then gently push in the rest as soon as you can.

4 ▲ Drain the pasta well in a colander, shaking it vigorously to remove all excess water. Serve immediately because the pasta will continue to cook in its own heat.

When to Undercook Pasta

If you are going to cook the pasta further, by baking it in a lasagne for example, undercook it slightly at this first stage. Pasta for a salad should also be a little undercooked, so that it will not become soggy when it is mixed with the dressing.

MAKING PASTA DOUGH

Pasta dough is very simple to make and, like most things, the more you do it the better the results will be. As in making pastry and bread doughs, the quantity of liquid needed can vary, according to how absorbent the flour is. The recipe here is for a basic egg pasta, with several variations.

MAKES ABOUT 1 POUND

1½ cups unbleached flour
1 teaspoon salt
2 extra large eggs, beaten to mix

1 ▲ Put the flour and salt on a work surface and make a well in the center. Add the eggs to the well.

2 ▲ With fingertips, gradually incorporate the flour into the eggs. When all the flour is mixed in, you should be able to gather up a pliable dough; if too moist, add more flour.

Pasta Flavorings
- For *Green Pasta*: Blanch ¾ pound of spinach, Swiss chard, or other greens, then drain well and squeeze dry. Purée or mince very finely. Add with the eggs.
- For *Fresh Herb Pasta*: Mince 1 cup loosely packed fresh herb leaves, such as basil, flat-leaf (Italian) parsley, and coriander (cilantro). Add with the eggs.
- For *Tomato Pasta*: Add 1½ tablespoons tomato paste with the eggs.
- For *Lemon Pasta*: Add 1½ tablespoons grated lemon rind with the eggs.
- For *Herb and Garlic Pasta*: Add ¼ cup minced parsley and oregano or marjoram and 1–2 minced garlic cloves with the eggs.
- For *Saffron Pasta*: Add ½ teaspoon ground saffron to the flour and salt or dissolve ½ teaspoon saffron threads in 1 tablespoon very hot water and add with the eggs through a small strainer.
- For *Whole-Wheat Pasta*: Substitute ½–1 cup whole-wheat flour for the same quantity of all-purpose flour.

3 ▲ Flour the work surface. Knead the dough by pushing it away with the heel of your hand and then folding it back. Continue kneading until it is smooth and elastic, 8–10 minutes. Or, use a pasta machine for kneading.

4 ▲ Shape the dough into a ball and put it in a bowl. Cover with plastic wrap. Let it rest at least 30 minutes before rolling and cutting.

Food Processor Pasta Dough
To mix the pasta dough in a food processor, put the flour and salt in the container. Pulse to blend. With the machine running, gradually add the eggs through the feed tube. Continue processing until the dough comes together into a ball that is smooth and elastic, 3–5 minutes.

ROLLING AND CUTTING PASTA DOUGH BY HAND

You can roll pasta dough by hand, but it is hard work. So if you intend to make pasta frequently, it is worth buying a machine.

Divide the dough into 3 or 4 pieces. Roll and cut one piece at a time. Keep the remaining dough tightly wrapped in plastic to prevent it from drying out while you work.

Pasta with Ham and Peas
Cook 2 minced garlic cloves in 2 tablespoons of butter in a medium saucepan until softened, about 3 minutes. Add 1 cup thawed frozen peas, ½ pound cooked ham cut into matchstick strips, 1 cup whipping cream, and seasoning, and bring to a boil. Toss with 1 pound thinly cut fresh pasta, cooked and drained, and ½ cup freshly grated Parmesan cheese. Serve immediately, with more cheese if desired. *Serves 4.*

Keeping Fresh Pasta
If fresh noodles are not to be cooked the day they are made, allow them to dry completely. Then wrap loosely and store at room temperature for up to 4 days.

1 ▲ Put a piece of dough on a lightly floured surface and pat it into a flat disk. Using a long rolling pin, roll out the dough in all directions, starting from the center each time.

3 ▲ For stuffed pasta shapes, use the dough immediately, while it is still malleable. If cutting noodles, sprinkle the rolled-out dough with flour and let it dry 10–15 minutes.

5 ▲ Uncoil the noodles with your fingers and scatter them on a floured dish towel. Let dry about 5 minutes before cooking. Or, wrap in plastic wrap and refrigerate for later cooking.

2 ▲ Continue rolling, with long even strokes, until you have a large sheet of dough that is about ⅛-inch thick, or less for thinner noodles.

4 ▲ To cut, roll up the sheet of dough like a flat jelly roll. With a knife, cut across the roll into noodles of the required width (⅛ inch for fettuccine, ¼ inch for tagliatelle).

6 ▲ To dry, leave them on the floured towel, or hang them over a broom handle, and let dry 2–3 hours. Sprinkle them with cornmeal to prevent them sticking together and pack loosely in a plastic bag or in a box with each layer separated.

USING A PASTA MACHINE

A pasta machine – hand-cranked or electric – takes all the drudgery out of making fresh pasta. You are able to roll the dough paper-thin and to cut very fine noodles such as tagliolini and tagliarini (1/16-inch width).

The smooth rollers on a pasta machine can be set wide apart or very close together, normally with the use of a dial. You start at the widest setting to knead the dough and then reduce the space gradually until the dough reaches the right thickness. Then a roller with blades cuts noodles of the desired width.

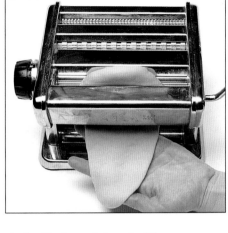

1 ▲ To knead dough: Flatten one piece of dough slightly and then feed it through the machine's rollers on their widest setting.

2 ▲ Fold the resulting strip of dough in half and feed it through again. Continue folding the dough and feeding it through until smooth and elastic, 8–10 times. (If it feels sticky, dust it with flour before continuing.)

Lemon Pasta with Clam Sauce
Cook 3 minced garlic cloves in 5 tablespoons of olive oil until softened, about 3 minutes. Add 1½ cups steamed shucked clams, chopped if large, with 3 tablespoons of their cooking liquid, or 2 (7-ounce) cans chopped cooked clams, drained. Heat the clams through; add ¼ cup chopped fresh parsley and 2–3 tablespoons lemon juice. Toss the sauce with 1 pound lemon pasta, cooked and drained, and plenty of freshly ground pepper. Serve immediately. *Serves 4.*

3 ▲ To roll dough: Adjust the rollers to the next narrower setting and feed the strip of dough through again, without folding it. Narrow the rollers again and feed the strip of dough through. Continue feeding the dough through the rollers at increasingly narrow settings until it is the desired thinness. Sprinkle with flour and let dry 10–15 minutes.

4 ▲ To cut noodles: Set the blades on the machine to the desired width. Feed the strip of dough through the blades, letting it fall onto a floured dish towel. Let dry about 5 minutes before cooking. Or dry completely for longer storage.

Drying Before Cutting
It is important to let the pasta dough dry out a bit before cutting it into noodles, or they will tend to stick together. If the day is humid, this initial drying can take up to 30 minutes.

CUTTING FLAT PASTA SHAPES

For wide noodles like pappardelle, and pasta for layering or rolling up such as lasagne and cannelloni, roll the dough by hand or machine to about ⅛-inch thickness. Lay the rolled dough strip, which will be about 4–5 inches wide, on a lightly floured surface. Trim the sides to make them straight and square with a sharp knife, or, for pappardelle, with a fluted pastry wheel. Lasagne may also be cut with a wheel for a decorative fluted edge.

1 ▲ To make lasagne or cannelloni: For lasagne, cut the dough strip into rectangles that are about 10–12 inches long, or of a size to fit your baking dish. For cannelloni, cut into smaller rectangles, about 3- × 5-inches.

2 ▲ For pappardelle: Cut the strip of dough into long noodles about ⅝-inch wide. Pappardelle are traditionally cut with a fluted pastry wheel, and need not be uniform as they are meant to have a rustic quality.

Tuna Lasagne

SERVES 6

1 quantity fresh pasta dough, cut for lasagne, or ¾ pound dry lasagne
1 tablespoon butter
1 small onion, minced
1 garlic clove, minced
¼ pound mushrooms, thinly sliced
¼ cup dry white wine (optional)
2½ cups white sauce
½ cup heavy whipping cream
3 tablespoons minced parsley
salt and pepper
2 7-ounce cans tuna, drained and flaked
2 canned pimientos, well drained, seeded, and cut into strips
½ cup thawed frozen peas
¾ cup shredded mozzarella
⅓ cup freshly grated Parmesan cheese

1 Bring a large pot of salted water to a boil. Add one-third of the lasagne noodles, one at a time, and cook until almost tender to the bite. Lift the noodles out with a slotted spatula into a colander and rinse with cold water.

2 ▲ Lay them on a dish towel, in one layer, to drain. Cook remaining noodles the same way, in 2 batches.

3 Preheat the oven to 350°F.

4 ▲ Melt the butter in a saucepan. Cook the onion until soft. Add the garlic and mushrooms. Cook until they are soft, stirring occasionally.

5 Pour in the wine, if using. Boil 1 minute. Add the white sauce, cream, and parsley. Season to taste.

6 Spoon a thin layer of sauce over the bottom of a 9- × 12-inch baking dish. Cover with a layer of lasagne noodles. Scatter half of the tuna, pimientos, peas, and shredded mozzarella over the noodles. Spoon one-third of the remaining sauce evenly over the top and cover with another layer of lasagne noodles.

7 ▲ Repeat the layers, ending with noodles and sauce. Sprinkle with the Parmesan. Bake until bubbling hot and the top is lightly browned, 35–40 minutes. Cut into large squares and serve from the baking dish.

COOKING RICE

There are many different ways to cook rice, and each has its adherents. The simplest is to cook rice in a large quantity of boiling water, then drain. However, valuable nutrients will be discarded in the water. The ways given here retain the rice's nutrients. Timings are for long-grain rice (one part rice to two parts water).

Rice Salad
Steam or bake 1 cup long-grain rice. While hot, dress with 6 tablespoons vinaigrette (page 182). Let cool. Add ½ cup each chopped scallions, celery, radishes, cucumber, and quartered black olives with another ½ cup vinaigrette. Toss well and sprinkle with chopped parsley. *Serves 4–6.*

2 ▲ To sauté and steam rice (pilaf): Heat oil, butter, or a mixture of the two in a saucepan over medium heat. Add the rice and stir to coat the grains. Sauté 2–3 minutes, stirring constantly. Add the measured quantity of boiling salted water. Bring back to a boil, then cover and steam over very low heat until the water has been absorbed and the rice is tender.

1 ◄ To steam rice: Put the measured quantity of salted water in a saucepan and bring to a boil. Add the rice and stir. Bring back to a boil, then cover the pan and steam over very low heat until the rice has absorbed all the water and is tender, 15–18 minutes for white rice and 35–40 minutes for brown rice. Remove the pan from the heat and let stand 5 minutes. Before serving, fluff the rice with a fork.

3 ▲ To bake rice: Put the rice in a baking dish and add the measured quantity of boiling salted water. Cover tightly with foil or a lid and bake in a preheated 350°F oven until the water has been absorbed and the rice is tender, 20–30 minutes for white rice and 35–45 for brown. Cooking time depends on many factors, including the seal of the dish.

A LOOK AT RICE

There are thousands of varieties of rice grown all over the world, with differing flavors and aromas. But for the cook, the choice of which rice to use in a dish is based mainly on the length of the rice grain.

Long-grain rice has grains that are four to five times as long as they are wide. It is dry and fluffy after cooking, with the grains remaining separate. Examples of long-grain rice include: Basmati (aromatic, with a rich nutty flavor; much used in Indian cooking), brown long-grain rice (husk removed but nutritious bran layer left; texture is slightly chewy, mild nutty flavor), and white or polished long-grain rice (most widely used; mild in flavor). Long-grain rice is excellent steamed or baked, in pilafs, and salads.

Short-grain rice, with an almost round shape, is very starchy and tends to cling together after cooking. Examples of short-grain rice include: Arborio rice (it gives a creamy texture to dishes) and glutinous or sweet rice (very sticky after cooking; used in Asian desserts and snacks). Short-grain rice is the one to use for puddings, risotto, croquettes, sushi, stir-fried rice, and molded rice dishes.

Medium-grain rice, in between the other two, is more tender than long-grain rice but less moist than short-grain. It is fluffy and separate if served hot, but clumps as it cools.

COOKING WILD RICE

Although called "rice," this is actually an aquatic grass. Its deliciously nutty flavor and firm, chewy texture make it a perfect complement to many meat and poultry dishes. It is also an excellent partner for vegetables such as winter squashes and mushrooms. It can be cooked like rice, by boiling or steaming, needing only a longer cooking time.

1 ▲ To boil wild rice: Add the rice to a large pot of boiling salted water (about 1 quart water to each cup of rice). Bring back to a gentle boil and cook until the rice is tender but still firm and has begun to split open, 45–50 minutes. Drain well.

2 ▲ To steam wild rice: Put the rice in a saucepan with the measured quantity of salted water. Bring to a boil, cover, and steam over very low heat until the rice is tender, 45–50 minutes. Cook uncovered for the last 5 minutes to evaporate excess water.

Wild Rice and Turkey Salad

SERVES 4

1 cup wild rice, boiled or steamed

2 celery stalks, thinly sliced

½ cup chopped scallions

¼ pound small button mushrooms, quartered

4 cups diced cooked turkey breast

½ cup vinaigrette dressing, made with walnut oil (page 182)

1 teaspoon fresh thyme leaves

2 pears, peeled, halved, and cored

¼ cup walnut pieces, toasted

1 ▲ Combine the cooked wild rice, celery, scallions, mushrooms, and turkey in a bowl.

2 ◄ Add the dressing and thyme and toss to coat thoroughly.

3 Thinly slice the pear halves lengthwise, without cutting through the stem end, and spread the slices like a fan. Divide the salad among 4 plates. Garnish with fanned pear halves and walnuts.

PREPARING LEGUMES

Legumes – beans, peas, and lentils – are a high-protein food. They keep well, making them a useful pantry staple. Most dried legumes require the same initial preparation.

An Extra Safeguard
To remove potentially harmful toxins when cooking dried beans, boil, uncovered, for 10 minutes before reducing the heat to a simmer for the rest of the time.

1 ▲ First rinse the legumes and pick out any small stones.

2 ▲ **To soak dried beans and peas**: Put them in a bowl, cover with plenty of cold water, and let soak at least 4 hours. (Lentils do not need soaking.)

3 ▲ A quick alternative method is to put the dried beans or peas in a large pan of water, bring to a boil and boil 2 minutes, then let soak 1 hour.

4 ▲ In either case, drain the legumes and rinse them well. They are now ready for cooking as the recipe directs.

5 ▲ **To cook**: Put the soaked and drained beans or peas or the lentils in a pan of fresh cold water (3 parts water to 1 part legumes) and bring to a boil. Then cover the pan, reduce the heat, and simmer until tender.

A LOOK AT LEGUMES

Dried beans, peas, and lentils range widely in color, shape, and size. They are endlessly versatile.

Some of the most commonly available beans include: **Great Northern**, small to medium-sized, kidney-shaped, white; **kidney**, medium-sized, kidney-shaped, smooth, shiny, may be reddish-brown or white (called cannellini beans); **navy**, small, oval, smooth, off-white; **black** (also called turtle beans), which are small, oval, smooth, shiny, jet-black; **pinto**, small, oval, smooth, beige with brown specks.

Other legumes include: **black-eyed peas**, small, oval, smooth, creamy color, with small cream-centered black dot in center on one side; **chickpeas** (also called garbanzo beans), medium-sized, round, not smooth, beige-tan; **peas**, small, round, or split in half, may be gray-green or yellow; **lentils**, tiny, disk-shaped, smooth, may be brownish-green, reddish-orange, or yellow.

All legumes are easy to prepare, and they can be used in all sorts of ways – in casseroles, soups, stews, purées, and salads.

The minimum soaking time for dried legumes is 4 hours, but they can be soaked overnight if that is more convenient. Lentils do not need soaking, and it is not essential for split peas, although they may be soaked to speed cooking.

Most dried legumes require about 1½–2 hours' cooking time. This includes black beans, pinto beans, navy beans, Great Northern beans, kidney beans, and chickpeas. Black-eyed peas and split peas require less time, about 1–1¼ hours. Lentils cook in less than ½ hour.

PREPARING BULGUR WHEAT

Bulgur wheat, a nutritious grain, is made by steaming whole wheat berries and then drying and cracking them into very small pieces. Cook like rice, either steamed plain or as a pilaf, or soak it to rehydrate. Serve as an accompaniment or use in salads.

Cooking Simple Bulgur Pilaf
Soften 1 small minced onion in 2 tablespoons butter. Add 1 cup bulgur wheat, 2 cups chicken stock, and a bay leaf. Cover and steam. To serve, season and stir in 2 tablespoons minced parsley.

1 ▲ **To steam bulgur:** Use two parts water to one part bulgur. Put the bulgur in a saucepan with water or other liquid such as stock, add flavorings if directed, and bring to a boil. Cover and simmer over low heat until tender, 12–15 minutes.

2 ▲ **To soak bulgur:** Put the bulgur in a strainer and rinse under cold running water until the water runs clear. Put the bulgur in a bowl, cover with fresh cold water, and let soak 1 hour until plump. Drain well, pressing out all excess moisture.

Bulgur Wheat Salad with Herbs

SERVES 6

¾ cup bulgur wheat, soaked and drained

1 cup seeded and diced ripe tomatoes

½ cup chopped red onion

¼ cup chopped scallions

1 cup minced parsley

¼ cup chopped fresh mint

½ cup olive or salad oil

⅓ cup lemon juice

salt and pepper

black olives and mint leaves, for garnishing

1 ▲ Combine all the ingredients in a large bowl.

2 ◄ Stir to mix the ingredients thoroughly. Taste and adjust the seasoning, adding more salt and pepper if needed.

3 Serve the salad at room temperature, garnished with black olives and mint leaves, if desired.

VEGETABLES

~

Using the wide variety of fresh vegetables available today, this vegetable primer shows preparation techniques and the different cooking methods suitable for each one. There are creative recipes, serving ideas and a method for making stock.

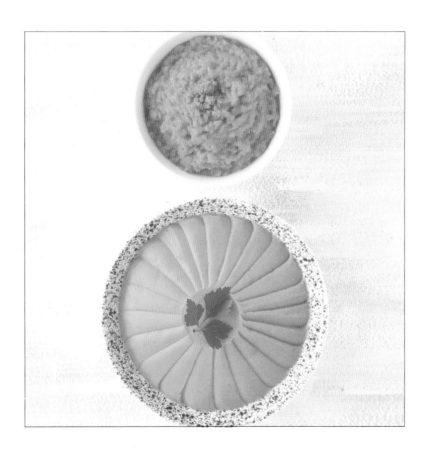

PREPARING AND COOKING VEGETABLES

To enjoy their full flavor, fresh vegetables are often best prepared and served simply. The following guidelines for vegetable preparation and cooking will help you make the most of seasonal bounty.

Season all vegetables to taste. Suggested amounts of raw prepared vegetable per portion are found with Serving Ideas. Recipes serve 4.

ROOTS AND BULBS
Carrots
Naturally sweet, carrots are used in innumerable dishes, both hot and cold, raw and cooked.

Preparation: If they are young, there is no need to peel them; just trim the ends and scrub well. Larger, older carrots should be peeled. Leave them whole or cut as directed. If carrots have a woody core, cut it out.

Cooking: *To boil*, drop into boiling salted water, then simmer until just tender: 8–10 minutes for whole baby carrots, 10–20 minutes for larger whole carrots, 4–10 minutes for sliced or grated carrots. *To steam*, cook whole baby carrots, covered, in a steamer over boiling water about 10 minutes. *To braise*, cook whole baby carrots or thinly sliced carrots with 3 tablespoons stock or water and 2 tablespoons butter per pound, tightly covered, for about 5 minutes. Boil, uncovered, to evaporate excess liquid before serving.

Serving Ideas (4 ounces per portion)
● Dress hot carrots with butter and chopped fresh herbs such as parsley, chives, thyme, or marjoram.
● Add a little sugar or honey and a squeeze of lemon or orange juice when braising. Or, try spices such as nutmeg, ginger, or curry powder.
● Serve raw carrot sticks with a dip.

Parsnips
Their sweet, nutty flavor makes a delicious addition to soups and stews or enjoy them on their own.

Preparation: Trim the ends and peel thinly. Leave small parsnips whole; cut up larger ones. If large parsnips have a woody core, cut it out.

Cooking: *To roast*, blanch in boiling salted water, then put in a roasting pan with butter or oil and cook in a preheated 400°F oven about 40 minutes. Baste occasionally. *To boil*, drop in boiling salted water, then simmer until just tender, 5–10 minutes. *To fry*, blanch in boiling water 1–2 minutes and drain. Fry in butter until golden brown and tender, 10–12 minutes.

Serving Ideas (4–5 ounces per portion)
● Add 4 tablespoons butter and ¼ cup honey to 1¼ pounds boiled parsnips; cook, covered, 5 minutes.
● Sauté sliced parsnips with sliced carrots; sprinkle with minced herbs.
● Bake 1¼ pounds small parsnips with ½ cup orange juice and 3 tablespoons butter, covered, in a preheated 350°F oven for 1 hour.
● Roast blanched parsnips in the pan around a roast of beef or pork.

Turnips
Mildly piquant, turnips go well with both sweet and savory seasonings.

Preparation: Trim the ends and peel the turnips thinly.

Cooking: *To steam*, cook cubes, covered, in a steamer over boiling water until tender, about 15 minutes. *To boil*, drop into boiling salted water and simmer until tender: 20–30 minutes for small whole turnips, about 7 minutes for diced. *To braise*, cook thin slices with 2 tablespoons butter and ⅓ cup stock or water per pound, covered tightly, for 4–5 minutes.

Serving Ideas (4 ounces per portion)
- Mash boiled turnips with milk and butter; mix with an equal quantity of mashed carrots, parsnips, or potatoes.
- Cover 1 pound steamed turnips with 2 cups hot white sauce. Top with bread crumbs and shredded cheese; brown under the broiler.
- Add sugar (1 tablespoon per pound) when braising turnips; uncover and boil to evaporate excess liquid and to caramelize the turnips.

Rutabaga

The orangey-yellow flesh of this root vegetable is sweet and full of flavor.

Preparation: Peel, removing all tough skin and roots. Cut as recipe directs.

Cooking: *To boil*, drop chunks into boiling salted water, then simmer until tender, 15 minutes. Do not overcook or the vegetable will be watery and mushy. *To steam*, cook slices or cubes, covered, in a steamer over boiling water until tender, about 10 minutes. *To braise*, cook with 2 tablespoons butter and ⅓ cup stock or water per pound, covered, for 5–7 minutes. *To roast*, put chunks or sticks around roasting meat and coat with the drippings. Roast at 400°F for about 45 minutes according to size.

Serving Ideas (5 ounces per portion)
- Braise 1¼ pounds grated rutabaga seasoned with 1 tablespoon brown sugar and 1 teaspoon soy sauce.
- Mash 1¼ pounds boiled rutabaga until smooth; beat in 2 eggs, ¼ cup whipping cream, 2 tablespoons flour, and ¼ teaspoon nutmeg until fluffy. Bake in a buttered dish in a preheated 350°F oven about 30 minutes.

Potatoes

Boiling potatoes are moist with a waxy texture so they keep their shape when cooked. Baking potatoes are dry and starchy and their texture is more mealy after cooking. In addition, there are orange-fleshed sweet potatoes, often called yams.

Preparation: If the potato skins will be eaten, scrub them well. Otherwise, peel potatoes.

Cooking: *To bake*, prick skins all over with a fork and bake in a preheated 400°F oven until tender, 1–1½ hours or 30–40 minutes for sweet potatoes. *To boil*, put in a pan of cold salted water, bring to a boil, then simmer until just tender, 10–20 minutes according to size. *To roast*, blanch peeled potatoes 1–2 minutes; drain and pat dry. Put in pan around

roasting meat and turn to coat with drippings; roast 1–1½ hours, turning occasionally. *To fry*, boil until partly cooked (unpeeled, if recipe directs), then fry slices or cubes in butter or oil until brown and crisp.

To deep fry (French fries), cut in sticks and soak in cold water at least 30 minutes; drain and pat dry. Fry (in small batches) in oil heated to 375°F until beginning to color, 3–7 minutes according to size. Drain on paper towels, then fry again until golden brown and crisp, about 3 minutes.

Stuffed Twice-Baked Potatoes
Cut baked potatoes in half lengthwise and scoop out the flesh, leaving a thin wall of flesh. Mash the scooped-out flesh with a little butter and 3 tablespoons each shredded Cheddar cheese and diced cooked ham per potato. Season to taste. Fill the potato shells with the mixture, mounding it. Sprinkle the tops with a little grated Cheddar, then bake at 400°F for 10–15 minutes.

Serving Ideas (6 ounces per portion)
- Dress boiled new potatoes with butter and minced mixed parsley and mint or toasted pine nuts.
- Mash boiled or baked sweet potatoes with an electric mixer. Add butter, salt and pepper to taste, orange juice to moisten, and a little ground cinnamon. Beat well.

Celery Root

The coarse knobby appearance of celery root, or celeriac, belies its delicate and delicious flavor.

Preparation: Peel off the thick skin. Do this just before cooking because celery root discolors when cut. If serving it raw, drop the peeled root or pieces into water acidulated with lemon juice or vinegar. Cut as directed in recipe.

Cooking: *To steam*, cook cubes, covered, in a steamer over boiling water until tender. *To boil*, drop cubes into boiling salted water, then simmer, covered, until just tender, 5–15 minutes according to size. *To braise*, cook grated celery root with 4 tablespoons butter and 2 tablespoons stock or water per pound, covered, for 5 minutes. Uncover and boil to evaporate excess liquid.

Serving Ideas (5 ounces per portion)
- Dress matchsticks of raw celery root with spicy mayonnaise and sprinkle with shreds of salami.
- Boil slices of celery root in beef stock; drain. Sprinkle with grated Parmesan cheese and serve hot.

Onions

The onion is one of those ingredients basic to almost every savory dish. There are pungent round onions and sweet mild onions: flat ones, large spherical ones (Spanish-type), and elongated Italian red ones. In addition, there are small boiling and pearl onions, shallots, and scallions (also called green onions).

Preparation: Peel off the papery skin. Then slice, chop, mince, etc., as the recipe directs. For scallions, trim the root end and cut off any wilted or discolored green leaves. Cut as directed, using just the white bulbs or both white and green parts.

Cooking: *To fry*, cook chopped or sliced onions, uncovered, in butter and/or oil over medium heat, stirring occasionally, until translucent and soft, about 5 minutes. If directed, continue cooking until the onions are golden brown. *To slow-cook or sweat*, cook sliced or chopped onions, covered, in butter and/or oil over low heat, stirring occasionally, until very soft and uniformly golden, about 30 minutes. *To boil* small onions, drop into boiling salted water, then simmer until tender, 15–20 minutes.

Serving Ideas
- Top hamburgers or hot dogs with slow-cooked sliced onions. (½ pound makes about ½ cup, cooked)
- Combine 1 pound boiled small onions with 3 tablespoons butter and ⅓ cup firmly packed light brown sugar; cook over low heat, stirring, until caramelized, about 10 minutes.
- Trim all but 2 inches of green from scallions. Stir-fry in hot oil and sprinkle with soy sauce.
- Use thin slices of sweet and red onions raw in salads.
- Bake whole onions in a 425°F oven until tender, about 45 minutes.

Leeks

This sweet and subtle member of the onion family has so many uses – both as a vegetable on its own and as a flavoring in soups, stews, and so on.

Preparation: Trim the root end and the dark green leaves, leaving just the pale green and white. (Save the dark green leaves for the stockpot.) Unless the leeks are to be cooked whole, slit them open lengthwise, to the center. Soak them in cold water for about 20 minutes. Drain well, shaking and squeezing out the excess water. If leeks are to be sliced or chopped, do this before rinsing them thoroughly in a colander under cold running water.

Cooking: *To braise,* cook with 2 tablespoons butter and ⅓ cup stock or water per pound, covered, until just tender. *To boil,* drop into boiling salted water or stock, then simmer until tender, 10–15 minutes. *To steam,* cook sliced or whole baby leeks, covered, in a steamer over boiling water until tender, 5–7 minutes.

Serving Ideas (6 ounces per portion)
● Boil whole leeks. Marinate while warm in a vinaigrette dressing; serve cool, not cold.
● Toss hot sliced leeks with butter and fresh herbs such as sage, tarragon, thyme, or parsley.
● Wrap whole boiled leeks in slices of ham. Cover with cheese sauce, sprinkle with grated cheese, and broil until the top is golden.

FRUITING VEGETABLES
Eggplant
The most familiar eggplants are the large ones with shiny purple skins, but there are also small round ones and long, thin ones, ranging in color from creamy white to deep violet. All can be used interchangeably.

Preparation: Trim off the stem end. Leave the eggplant whole or cut according to recipe directions.

Cooking: *To broil,* brush cut surfaces with oil. Broil, 3–4 inches from the heat, until tender and well browned, about 10 minutes total; turn once and brush with oil. *To fry,* coat slices or thick sticks with flour or dip in batter, if recipe directs, then pan-fry in hot oil or butter until golden, about 5 minutes on each side. *To braise,* brown slices or wedges in a little hot oil, add ¼ cup stock or water per pound, cover, and cook until tender, about 12 minutes total. Add more liquid if necessary. *To bake,* prick whole eggplant all over with a fork. Bake in a preheated 400°F oven until soft, about 20 minutes.

Serving Ideas (5 ounces per portion)
● Baste broiled or grilled eggplant with garlic- or herb-flavored olive oil.
● Braise eggplant, adding 2 peeled, chopped tomatoes and ¼ cup chopped fresh basil.
● Serve fried flour-coated eggplant with garlic mayonnaise.

Summer Squashes
Thin-skinned squashes, such as zucchini, pattypan, and crookneck, are completely edible, skin and all.

Preparation: Trim the ends from summer squash. Cut as directed.

Cooking: *To fry* sliced summer squash, cook in butter or oil until tender and golden brown, 5–10 minutes. *To boil,* drop in boiling salted water, then simmer until tender: 10–12 minutes if whole, 3–8 minutes if sliced. *To steam,* cook, covered, in a steamer over boiling water until tender. *To braise,* cook sliced squash, with 2 tablespoons butter and ⅓ cup stock or water per pound, tightly covered, until tender, 4–5 minutes.

Serving Ideas (5 ounces per portion)
● Sauté sliced summer squash with minced garlic and chopped fresh parsley and oregano.
● Cut small zucchini in half lengthwise and spread cut surfaces with grainy mustard. Broil about 4 inches from the heat until crisp-tender, about 5 minutes.

Winter squashes
Acorn, butternut, and hubbard squashes, and pumpkin have a hard rind and central seeds and fibers that should be removed before cooking.

Preparation: Unless baking in the skin, peel winter squash with a large, sturdy knife. Scrape away the seeds and stringy fibers.

Cooking: *To steam*, cook cubes, covered, in a steamer over boiling water until tender. *To bake*, cut in serving pieces, leaving on the rind, and score the flesh. Arrange cut-side up in greased baking dish, dot with butter, and bake in a preheated 375°F oven until tender, about 45 minutes. *To boil*, drop pieces in boiling salted water, then simmer until tender, 4–5 minutes. *To braise*, cook cubes of winter squash as for summer squash.

Serving Ideas (5–8 ounces per portion)
● Add 1 diced apple, a squeeze of lemon juice, and 2 tablespoons brown sugar when braising 1¼ pounds winter squash. If desired, spice with a little cinnamon, nutmeg, or curry powder.
● Bake acorn squash halves with 1 teaspoon maple syrup in each.

LEAFY, GREEN, AND OTHER VEGETABLES
Spinach
Small tender leaves have a delicate flavor and can be used raw in salads. Large, strongly flavored, darker leaves taste better cooked.

Preparation: Spinach can hide a lot of grit so needs careful rinsing. Immerse in cold water, swish around, and let

soak 3–4 minutes. Then lift out the spinach and immerse in fresh cold water. Repeat, then drain in a colander. Discard any damaged or yellowed leaves. Pull off tough stems.

Cooking: *To steam-boil*, put in a large pan (there should be sufficient water left on the leaves after rinsing so that no more is needed). Cook until just wilted, 5–7 minutes, stirring occasionally to help evaporate the liquid. Drain well and press the spinach between two plates or squeeze in your fist. *To braise*, cook with 2 tablespoons butter per pound, covered, until wilted. Uncover and boil to evaporate excess liquid. *To stir-fry*, cook small or shredded leaves in hot oil until just wilted, 3–5 minutes.

Serving Ideas (6 ounces per portion)
● Add ¼ cup whipping cream and ¼ teaspoon grated nutmeg to 1¼ pounds braised spinach.
● Stir-fry minced onion and garlic, then add spinach with halved cherry tomatoes and stir-fry 1 minute.
● Steam-boil spinach leaves; chop finely after draining. Fry in olive oil with minced garlic, stirring, until the garlic just starts to turn golden and the spinach is heated through.
● Combine equal parts of chopped cooked spinach and cooked rice with butter and seasoning to taste.

Greens
Hearty greens include those from the cabbage family – kale, collards, rape, mustard greens – as well as beet greens and Swiss chard. Serve alone, or add them to soups and stews.

Preparation: Discard damaged or yellowed leaves. Trim off root ends and large or coarse stems. Leave the leaves whole or shred, according to recipe directions. Cut leaves from stems of Swiss chard and cook separately (the stems take longer).

Cooking: *To braise*, put shredded leaves (or Swiss chard stems) in a pan with 2 tablespoons butter and 3 tablespoons stock per pound. Cook, covered, until just tender. Boil, uncovered, to evaporate excess liquid. *To steam-boil*, put in a large pan (there should be enough water left on the leaves after rinsing so no more is needed). Cover and cook until just wilted, 5–15 minutes according to variety. *To boil*, drop shredded leaves (or Swiss chard stems) in boiling salted water, then simmer until just tender.

Serving Ideas (6–8 ounces per portion)
● Toss hot braised greens with whipping cream or sour cream and grated nutmeg; heat gently.
● Mix boiled greens with mashed potato. Shape into patties, coat in fine bread crumbs, and fry in butter until golden brown on both sides.
● Top boiled or braised greens with crisply fried bacon and shredded Swiss cheese; broil to melt the cheese.

Green Beans

Crisp green beans are available in varying sizes, from tiny French ones ("haricots verts") to very large ones, often called pole beans. Yellow versions are known as wax beans. Green beans are also called string (or stringless) beans, runner beans, or snap beans; Chinese long beans are similar, but longer.

Preparation: Snip off both ends with scissors or use a knife. For string beans, snap off the ends, pulling the strings from the sides as you do so. Cut large beans diagonally or sliver.

Cooking: *To boil*, drop into boiling salted water, then simmer until just tender but still crisp and bright green, 3–15 minutes, according to size. *To steam*, cook, covered, in a steamer over boiling water until tender. *To braise*, cook with ⅓ cup stock or water and 2 tablespoons butter per pound, tightly covered, until tender. *To stir-fry*, blanch in boiling water for 2 minutes; drain, refresh, and pat dry. Stir-fry in hot oil 2–3 minutes.

Serving Ideas (4 ounces per portion)
● Dress boiled or steamed beans with melted butter, chopped herbs, and a squeeze of lemon juice.

● Add ⅓ cup whipping cream per pound to braised beans. Cook, stirring, until the liquid has reduced and the beans are glazed.
● Top hot beans with quickly fried shreds of prosciutto. Or, top with sliced almonds or pecans lightly browned in butter.

Peas

Snow peas and sugar peas are completely edible, pod and all. Green or garden peas are removed from their pods for cooking; the pods weigh as much as the peas, so you need to allow twice as much as edible pod peas.

Preparation: If green peas are in the pod, split it open and pop out the peas. Snap off both ends from snow and sugar peas, pulling any tough strings from the sides as you do so.

Cooking: *To steam*, cook, covered, in a steamer over boiling water until tender. *To boil*, drop into boiling salted water, then simmer until just tender: 5–10 minutes for green peas, 1–2 minutes for snow and sugar peas. *To braise*, cook, covered, with 2 tablespoons butter and ¼ cup stock or water per pound, until tender: 5–10 minutes for green peas, 2 minutes for snow and sugar peas.

Serving Ideas (4 ounces per portion)
● Add sliced scallions, shredded lettuce, and a generous pinch of sugar when braising green peas.
● Stir-fry snow peas with thinly sliced onion and mushrooms.
● Add ¼ cup whipping cream to braised sugar peas and cook uncovered, stirring, until almost all liquid has evaporated.

Broccoli

Serve this green vegetable hot or let it cool and use in salads. It is also excellent in stir-fries.

Preparation: Trim off the end of the stem. If the rest of the stem is to be used in the recipe, peel it. According to recipe directions, leave the head whole or cut off the florets, or flowers, taking a little stem with each one. Cut the remainder of the peeled stem across in thin slices.

Cooking: *To steam*, cook, covered, in a steamer over boiling water until tender. *To boil*, drop into boiling salted water, then simmer until just tender: 7–12 minutes for heads, 4–6 minutes for florets and thinly sliced stems. *To braise*, cook with ⅓ cup stock and 2 tablespoons butter per pound, covered, until tender.

Serving Ideas (5 ounces per portion)
● Toss hot broccoli with a flavored butter.
● Cover hot broccoli with cheese sauce, sprinkle with grated Parmesan, and brown under broiler.
● Blanch small broccoli florets about 1 minute; drain and refresh. Serve cold, dressed with vinaigrette and sprinkled with toasted nuts.

Cauliflower

White or ivory cauliflower is the most widely available, although there are also green and purple varieties.

Preparation: Cut away the large green leaves, leaving only the tiny ones if desired. Trim the stem level and cut an "x" in the base or cut out the core. Leave the head whole, or break into florets before or after cooking.

Cooking: *To steam*, cook florets, covered, in a steamer over boiling water, 12–15 minutes. *To steam-boil*, put stem-down in a pan with about 1 inch boiling salted water and a bay leaf. Cover and cook until crisp-tender: 15–30 minutes for whole heads, 5–9 minutes for florets. Drain well. *To braise*, cook florets, with 3 tablespoons butter and ⅓ cup stock per pound, covered, for 5–7 minutes.

Serving Ideas (5–6 ounces per portion)
● Dress hot cauliflower with butter; sprinkle with chopped fresh chives or parsley, or toasted sliced almonds or chopped pecans.
● Top hot cauliflower with hollandaise sauce.
● Bread florets in egg and crumbs, then deep-fry and serve with garlic or spicy mayonnaise.

Cabbage

Rich in vitamins and very versatile, cabbage is good cooked or raw. Varieties include firm, round heads (green, white, and red), looser round heads (Savoy with its crinkly leaves), and long, loose heads (bok choy and Napa, Chinese, or celery cabbage).

Preparation: Discard any wilted or discolored outer leaves. Cut the heads into small wedges (or quarters for long, loose heads). Cut out the coarse stem from the wedges before cooking. Or, quarter heads and shred them. Leave long, loose heads whole and cut heads across the leaves to shred.

Cooking: *To braise*, quickly blanch chopped or shredded green, Savoy, or red cabbage. (There is no need to blanch Napa cabbage.) Cook green, Savoy, and Napa cabbage with ⅓ cup stock or water and 2 tablespoons butter per pound, tightly covered, for 3–4 minutes. For red cabbage, increase liquid by 1 cup and cook 30 minutes. *To boil*, drop into boiling salted water, then simmer until just crisp-tender: 6–8 minutes for wedges, 3–5 minutes for shredded green, Savoy, or Napa cabbage. *To steam*, cook, covered, in a steamer over boiling water until tender.

Serving Ideas (4 ounces per portion)
● Add chopped fresh dill when braising green or Savoy cabbage.
● Blanch larger outer leaves of green or Savoy cabbage, then roll them up around a ground meat stuffing and simmer in a rich tomato sauce.
● Add sliced apples, cooked diced bacon, and warm spices (cinnamon, nutmeg) when braising red cabbage.
● Use shredded Napa cabbage raw in tossed salads.

Cauliflower au Gratin
Cut a large cauliflower head into florets and steam until crisp-tender. Spread in a buttered gratin dish and scatter sautéed sliced mushrooms over the florets. Pour 2 cups hot cheese sauce evenly over the top and sprinkle with a mixture of grated Cheddar cheese and fine dry bread crumbs. Brown under the broiler. *Serves 4.*

Brussels Sprouts

These miniature heads of cabbage are best cooked just until crisp-tender.

Preparation: Remove any discolored leaves. Trim the stems level with the heads. If cooking whole, cut an "x" in the base of the stem so that it will cook in the same time as the head.

Cooking: *To braise*, cook with ⅓ cup stock or water and 2 tablespoons butter per pound, covered, until just tender, 8–10 minutes. *To boil*, drop into boiling salted water, then simmer until just tender, 7–10 minutes. *To steam*, cook, covered, in a steamer over boiling water for 10–12 minutes.

Serving Ideas (4 ounces per portion)
- Toss with butter and orange rind.
- Toss with toasted nuts, braised or poached chestnuts, or sliced canned water chestnuts.
- Cut the heads lengthwise in half and blanch in boiling water 2–3 minutes; drain and refresh. Stir-fry in hot oil with minced fresh ginger and garlic until tender and lightly browned, 2–3 minutes.
- Shred and blanch 2–3 minutes; drain and refresh. Add minced onion and celery and toss with a lemony vinaigrette dressing.

Celery

Crisp green celery is a popular salad ingredient and favorite flavoring in soups, stews, and stuffings.

Preparation: Separate the stalks. Scrub with a vegetable brush under cold running water. Trim off the root end, leaves, and any blemishes (keep leaves for the stockpot). If the stalks have tough strings, remove these with a vegetable peeler. Cut as directed. For celery hearts, cut in half lengthwise. Trim off the leaves.

Cooking: *To steam-boil*, put in a pan with 1 inch of boiling salted water. Cover and cook until crisp-tender: 5–10 minutes for pieces, 10–20 minutes for hearts. *To braise*, cook slices with 2 tablespoons stock or water and 2 tablespoons butter per ½ pound, or hearts with 1 cup liquid, covered, until tender: 3 minutes for thin slices, 10–20 minutes for hearts.

Serving Ideas (4 ounces per portion)
- Stuff finger-length pieces of raw celery with blue cheese, flavored cream cheese, or peanut butter.
- Sprinkle braised celery with chopped walnuts and minced parsley.
- Braise celery hearts with chopped tomatoes and tarragon or thyme.

Mushrooms

Cultivated or common mushrooms are widely available; you may also find fresh wild mushrooms such as shiitake, oyster, chanterelle, and enoki.

Preparation: Rinse or wipe with a damp paper towel (don't leave in water as mushrooms absorb liquid readily). Trim gritty stems; cut off tough stems of wild mushrooms. Small mushrooms can be left whole; larger ones are normally halved, quartered, or sliced, or they may be diced or minced as required. Pull stems from large mushrooms to be stuffed.

Cooking: *To fry*, cook in hot butter and/or oil until tender, about 4 minutes, stirring frequently. The mushrooms will give up liquid; if the recipe directs, continue frying until the liquid has evaporated and the mushrooms have browned. *To broil*, brush with melted butter and/or oil. Broil about 4 inches from the heat, turning and basting occasionally, until tender and browned, 5–8 minutes.

Serving Ideas (4 ounces per portion)
- Fry sliced mushrooms with minced garlic and thyme.
- Top broiled mushroom caps with a pat of flavored butter.

CHOPPING AND MINCING VEGETABLES

In countless recipes, vegetables and other ingredients need to be chopped to varying degrees of fineness. Very fine chopping is called mincing.

For most chopping, use a large, sharp chef's knife. You can also use a food processor, but take care not to over-process vegetables to a pulp.

Cheese and Herb Dip
Combine 1 cup cream cheese and 1 cup cottage cheese in a food processor or blender and blend until smooth. Turn the cheese mixture into a bowl and stir in 2 tablespoons minced fresh dill and ¾ cup minced chives. Season to taste with salt and pepper. If the dip is too thick, stir in a few spoonfuls of half-and-half or milk. Cover and chill for at least 1 hour before serving, with vegetables, crackers, or potato chips for dipping. *Makes 2½ cups.*

Peeling Whole Garlic
If you want to peel garlic and keep the clove whole, drop it into boiling water, count to 30, then drain and rinse with cold water. The skin will slip off easily.

1 ▲ To chop an onion: Peel it, leaving on the root end to hold the onion together. Cut it in half, straight through the root.

3 ▲ Make vertical lengthwise cuts in the onion half, again not cutting the root. Finally, cut across the onion to chop it, guiding the side of the knife with your knuckles. Discard the root.

5 ▲ Crush the peeled clove again with the knife to flatten it, then begin to chop it. When it is coarsely chopped, continue chopping and crushing it until it is finely minced. Hold the tip of the knife on the board and raise and lower the knife handle with your other hand, moving the blade back and forth over the garlic.

2 ▲ Put one half flat on the work surface and hold the onion steady at the root end. With a chef's knife, make horizontal cuts in the onion half to the root, but without cutting all the way through it.

4 ▲ To mince garlic: Set a chef's knife flat on top of the clove and bang it gently with the side of your fist to crush the garlic slightly and loosen the skin. Remove the skin.

6 ▲ To chop fresh herbs: Hold the leaves or sprigs together in a bunch and chop coarsely, then continue mincing as for garlic (without crushing). You can also use this method of mincing for vegetables and fresh ginger.

BLANCHING AND REFRESHING

Foods are blanched for several reasons: to loosen skins before peeling (tomatoes, peaches, and nuts), to set color and flavor (for vegetables before freezing), to reduce bitterness (in some vegetables), to firm flesh (sweetbreads), and to remove excess salt (country ham, bacon). Vegetables are often blanched as an initial cooking, when further cooking is to be done by stir-frying or a brief reheating in butter before serving, or if they are to be used in a salad. After blanching, most foods are "refreshed" to stop them cooking any further.

1 ▲ **To blanch:** Immerse the food in a large pan of boiling water (ideally use a wire basket or strainer so the food can be lifted out easily). Bring the water back to a boil and boil for the time directed, usually 1–2 minutes. Immediately lift the food out of the water (in its basket or with a slotted spoon or drain in a colander).

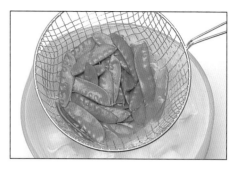

2 ▲ **To refresh:** Quickly immerse the food in ice water or hold under cold running water. If the recipe directs, leave until it has cooled completely. Drain well.

Broccoli, Cauliflower, and Carrot Salad

SERVES 4

1 small head of cauliflower, cut into florets and stems trimmed

½ pound broccoli, cut into florets and stems trimmed

2 carrots, thickly sliced

⅓ cup vegetable oil

¼ cup coarsely chopped almonds

2 tablespoons red wine vinegar

½ teaspoon ground cumin

salt and pepper

1 Blanch the cauliflower, broccoli, and carrots separately in boiling salted water, allowing 10 minutes for the cauliflower and 5 minutes for the broccoli and carrots. Drain well and refresh in ice water.

2 ▶ Heat 1 tablespoon of the oil in a small frying pan. Add the almonds. Fry until golden brown, about 5 minutes, stirring frequently. Drain on paper towels and let cool.

3 Combine the remaining oil with the vinegar, cumin, salt, and pepper in a large bowl. Whisk well together. Add the vegetables and toss to coat with the dressing. Scatter the almonds on top. Serve at room temperature.

SWEATING

Sweating is a common preliminary step in vegetable cooking, particularly for onions and leeks. This process, which is essentially a form of steaming, draws out the juices and develops the vegetable's flavor.

A Matter of Weight
Be sure the pan you use has a heavy base that will conduct the heat gently and evenly, or the vegetable may stick and burn. The cover should fit tightly to keep in all the moisture.

1 ▲ Heat fat (usually butter) over low heat in a heavy saucepan or frying pan that has a tight fitting lid. Add the vegetable and stir to coat with the melted fat.

2 ▲ Cover the pan tightly and cook gently until the vegetable is softened but not brown; onions will be translucent. This can take 10–15 minutes or longer. Uncover to stir occasionally during the cooking.

Pasta with Zucchini and Walnut Sauce

SERVES 4

5 tablespoons butter

1 large yellow onion, halved and thinly sliced

1 pound zucchini, very thinly sliced

¾ pound short pasta shapes such as penne, ziti, rotini, or fusilli

½ cup coarsely chopped walnuts

3 tablespoons minced fresh parsley

2 tablespoons half-and-half

salt and pepper

freshly grated Parmesan cheese, for serving

1 ▲ Melt the butter in a frying pan and add the onion. Cover and sweat for 5 minutes, then add the zucchini.

2 Stir well, cover again, and sweat until the vegetables are very soft, stirring occasionally.

3 Meanwhile, bring a large pot of salted water to a boil. Add the pasta to the boiling water, stir, and cook until it is just tender to the bite ("al dente"), about 10 minutes. Check the package directions for timing.

4 While the pasta is cooking, add the walnuts, parsley, and half-and-half to the zucchini mixture and stir well. Season to taste with salt and pepper.

5 Drain the pasta and return it to the pot. Add the zucchini sauce and mix well together. Serve immediately, with plenty of Parmesan cheese sprinkled on top.

MASHING AND PURÉEING

The smooth texture of a mashed or puréed vegetable is very appealing, perhaps because it reminds us of childhood food. Vegetables to be finished this way may be first boiled, steamed, sweated, or baked.

Carrot Purée
Thinly slice 1½ pounds carrots. Put them in a saucepan, cover with water, and add a pinch of salt. Bring to a boil and simmer until tender, 10–15 minutes. Drain well, then purée the carrots in a food processor. Add 2 tablespoons butter, ¼ cup each milk and orange juice, and ½ teaspoon ground cardamom or ⅛ teaspoon grated nutmeg. Season with salt and pepper. Reheat, stirring frequently. *Serves 4.*

Whipped Sweet Potatoes
Mash 1½ pounds boiled or baked sweet potatoes with an electric mixer. Add butter, ¼ cup orange juice, and ¼ teaspoon ground cinnamon; beat well.

1 ▲ To mash potatoes and sweet potatoes: Mash the warm, freshly cooked vegetables with a potato masher or put through a potato ricer. With a wooden spoon, beat in butter and milk, then season.

3 ▲ To purée other root vegetables and most squashes: Put the freshly cooked vegetable in a food processor and process until smooth, scraping down the sides of the container as necessary. Season to taste.

2 ▲ Alternatively, beat them with an electric mixer. A third method, less successful, is to use a potato masher. Do not use a food processor for puréeing starchy vegetables such as potatoes; it will make them gluey.

4 ▲ To purée vegetables with fibers: Use a vegetable mill for fibrous vegetables, such as green beans, legumes, or stringy squashes, unless you are prepared to push the food-processor purée through a strainer.

5 ◄ To purée greens: Remove the stems of leaves such as spinach or chard before cooking. Purée in a food processor. Be sure to squeeze out as much water as possible, both before and after puréeing, especially if adding cream. Season to taste.

MAKING VEGETABLE STOCK

Adapt the ingredients for this fresh-flavored stock to what you have on hand. Refrigerate, covered, for up to 5 days or freeze for up to 1 month.

MAKES ABOUT 2½ QUARTS

2 large onions, coarsely chopped

2 leeks, sliced

3 garlic cloves, crushed with the flat side of a knife

3 carrots, coarsely chopped

4 celery stalks, coarsely chopped

a large strip of lemon rind

a handful of parsley stems (about 12)

a few fresh thyme sprigs

2 bay leaves

2½ quarts water

1 ▲ Put the vegetables, strip of lemon rind, herbs, and water in a stockpot and bring to a boil. Skim off the foam that rises to the surface, doing so frequently at first, and then just from time to time.

2 ▲ Reduce the heat and simmer, uncovered, for 30 minutes. Strain the stock and let it cool.

Vegetable and Herb Chowder

SERVES 4

2 tablespoons butter

1 onion, minced

1 leek, thinly sliced

1 celery stalk, diced

1 bell pepper, yellow or green, seeded and diced

2 tablespoons minced fresh parsley

1 tablespoon flour

1 quart vegetable stock

¾ pound boiling potatoes, peeled and diced

a few fresh thyme sprigs, or ½ teaspoon dried thyme

1 bay leaf

¼ pound string beans, thinly sliced on the diagonal

½ cup milk

salt and pepper

1 ▲ Melt the butter in a heavy saucepan or Dutch oven and add the onion, leek, celery, bell pepper, and parsley. Cover and cook over low heat until the vegetables are soft.

2 Add the flour and stir until well blended. Add the stock slowly, stirring to combine. Bring to a boil, stirring frequently.

3 ▼ Add the potatoes, thyme, and bay leaf. Simmer, uncovered, about 10 minutes.

4 Add the beans and simmer until all the vegetables are tender, 10–15 minutes longer.

5 Stir in the milk. Season with salt and pepper. Heat through. Before serving, discard the thyme stems and bay leaf. Serve hot.

PREPARING SALAD GREENS

Crisp, fresh green and variegated leaves are very appetizing. Use them as the background for a vegetable, fish, meat, or fruit salad, or make the leaves the focus.

Lettuce

There are four main types of lettuce: crisphead, with solid heads of tightly packed, crisp leaves (iceberg); butterhead, with looser heads of soft-textured leaves (Bibb or limestone, Boston); romaine, with its elongated head of crisp leaves; and looseleaf, with leaves that do not form a head (salad bowl, oak leaf).

Preparation: Discard wilted or damaged leaves. Twist or cut out the central core. Rinse the leaves thoroughly in cold water and soak briefly to draw out any grit trapped in the folds. Drain and blot or spin dry. If the leaves are large, tear in pieces.

Other Salad Ingredients

To provide contrast in texture and flavor, add brightly colored and crunchy, sharp-flavored leaves, such as radicchio or red cabbage, with plain leaves. Cucumber, scallions, and carrot are also appealing in a mixed salad, as are raw or lightly cooked green beans or snow peas. Nuts or dried fruit are tasty additions, as are shredded or cubed cheese, or croutons.

Endive and Escarole

These members of the chicory family bring an appealing bitterness to salads. The smooth, pale leaves of Belgian endive are more delicate and sweet than those of curly endive (sometimes labeled chicory), which has frilly green leaves with a coarse texture. Escarole has broader, fleshier leaves with jagged edges and a firm texture.

Preparation: Trim the base and cut out the core. Discard wilted or damaged leaves. Rinse and dry the leaves. If large, tear in smaller pieces.

Lamb's Lettuce

Also know as corn salad or "mâche," this salad green has a pleasantly firm, chewy texture and mild, slightly nutty flavor. The leaves are small and may be spoon-shaped or round.

Preparation: Remove any wilted or damaged leaves. Trim roots. Rinse well, as the leaves can be sandy.

Arugula

In a salad of mixed greens, the pungent peppery, nutty taste of arugula is unmistakable and welcome. This member of the mustard family, also called rocket, has deep green leaves with curved edges and a texture somewhat like spinach.

Preparation: Discard any wilted or damaged leaves. Pull off roots. Rinse thoroughly and dry on paper towels – it's best not to use a salad spinner, which could bruise the leaves.

Watercress

Another member of the mustard family, the round dark green leaves have a wonderful peppery flavor that enlivens any salad, and the fresh, attractive appearance of watercress makes it a popular garnish.

Preparation: Discard wilted or damaged leaves and snap off thick stems. Rinse well and spin dry.

RINSING AND CRISPING SALAD GREENS

It is vital that all salad leaves be thoroughly rinsed to remove any grit or insects, as well as residues of sprays. Just as important is to dry the salad leaves thoroughly so that the dressing will not be diluted.

Lettuce with Blue Cheese Dressing
For each serving, use 1 small head of Bibb lettuce or heart of Boston lettuce, washed and spun or blotted dry. Top with 3–4 tablespoons blue cheese dressing. Garnish with cherry tomatoes and chives, if desired.

Salad Success
● Dress salad greens just before serving, otherwise the leaves will wilt and become unpleasantly soggy.
● Match the dressing to the greens: sharp leaves need hearty flavors, but the same dressing used on delicate greens would overpower them.
● Be imaginative with salad additions. A little crumbled goat cheese, for instance, can lift a plain salad, especially with a sprinkling of fresh herbs or nuts.

1 ▲ Discard any wilted, discolored, or damaged leaves. For spinach, watercress, and similar greens, pull off the stems. Trim off any roots.

3 ▲ Put the leaves in a sink or large bowl of cold water and swirl them around to wash off any dirt or insects. Let settle 1-2 minutes.

5 ▲ Alternatively, put the washed leaves in a salad spinner to spin off the water. (Do not use a salad spinner for leaves that bruise easily.)

2 ▲ For leaves in compact or loose heads, pull them individually from the core or stem.

4 ▲ Lift the leaves out of the water onto a dish towel and pat dry gently with paper towels or another dish towel.

6 ▲ Wrap the leaves loosely in a clean dish towel or paper towels and put in a large plastic bag. Refrigerate about 1 hour. When assembling the salad, tear any large leaves into smaller, bite-sized pieces.

EGGS

~

*Eggs are so versatile and this chapter shows how to make
perfect boiled, scrambled, fried, baked and poached eggs, as
well as describing techniques for turning eggs into batters
and crêpe mixtures.*

BOILING EGGS

The derisive expression, "can't boil an egg," indicates the importance of this basic cooking skill, although, to be accurate, eggs are simmered rather than boiled.

For many people, a soft-boiled egg with toast is a favorite breakfast. But the soft-boiled egg and its cousin the coddled egg have many delicious applications. If they are to be peeled for serving, cook them for the longest time suggested below. The salt in the cooking water aids in peeling.

Hard-boiled eggs make classic salads and sandwich fillings, as well as cold first course and buffet dishes and hot main dishes.

1 ▲ To hard-boil eggs: Bring a pan of well-salted water to a boil. Using a slotted spoon, lower each egg into the water. Reduce the heat so the water is just simmering gently. Cook 10 minutes. Immediately plunge the eggs into a bowl of ice water and let cool.

2 ▲ When the eggs are cool enough to handle, peel them. If they are not to be used immediately, keep the peeled eggs in a bowl of cold salted water. Or, store the eggs, still in the shell, in the refrigerator; they will keep up to 1 week.

Egg, Potato, and Bean Salad
Bring a pot of salted water to a boil. Add 1 pound small unpeeled new potatoes. Bring back to a boil and simmer 10 minutes. Add ½ pound thin green beans ("haricots verts") and simmer until the potatoes and beans are just tender, 4–5 minutes longer. Drain well in a colander and refresh under cold running water. Turn the vegetables into a large bowl. Sprinkle ¼ cup olive oil and 2 tablespoons balsamic vinegar over them. Season with salt and pepper and toss well. Scatter 2 grated hard-boiled eggs and 3 tablespoons coarsely shredded mixed fresh mint and basil over the top. Serve warm or at room temperature. *Serves 4–6.*

3 ▲ To coddle eggs: Lower them into a pan of boiling salted water. Cover the pan and remove it from the heat. Let stand until the eggs are done to your taste, 6–8 minutes. Lift out each egg and place it in an egg cup for serving; cut off the top of the shell so the egg can be scooped out. Or, plunge the eggs into a bowl of cold water and cool, then peel carefully. To reheat for serving, immerse in a bowl of hot water for 1–2 minutes.

Hard-Boiled Egg Tips
- Always cool hard-boiled eggs in ice water. The abrupt temperature change helps prevent a gray layer from forming around the egg yolk.
- To peel hard-boiled eggs, tap them gently on a hard surface to crack the shell. Carefully peel under cold running water.

4 ▲ To soft-boil eggs: Bring a pan of well-salted water to a boil. Using a slotted spoon, lower each egg into the water. Reduce the heat so the water just simmers. Cook until the eggs are done to your taste, 3–5 minutes (depending on how firm you like the white to be; the yolk will be runny).

Ideas for Soft-Boiled and Coddled Eggs
- For *Caviar-Crowned Eggs:* Cut the top ¾ inch from each egg, in its shell. Put a spoonful of sour cream and caviar on the egg.
- For *Smoked-Salmon Eggs:* Prepare as above and top each with a spoonful each of sour cream and diced smoked salmon.
- Put a hot peeled egg in the center of a bowl of cream of spinach or watercress soup.

SCRAMBLING EGGS

Tender, creamy scrambled eggs are perfect for breakfast or brunch, but you can also add flavorings for a more unusual snack or supper dish.

Ideas for Scrambled Eggs
- Add minced fresh herbs (chives, tarragon) to the beaten eggs.
- Cook diced vegetables (onions, mushrooms, bell peppers) or ham in the butter before adding the eggs.
- Stir in a little grated cheese or bits of cream cheese just before the eggs have finished cooking.
- Fold small cooked shelled shrimp into scrambled eggs.

1 ▲ Put the eggs in a bowl and add a little salt and pepper. Beat the eggs with a fork until they are well blended. Melt butter in a frying pan over medium-low heat (butter should cover the bottom of the pan generously). Pour in the beaten eggs.

2 ▲ Cook, scraping up and turning the eggs over, until they are softly set and still moist, 3–5 minutes. The eggs will continue to cook after being removed from the heat, so undercook them slightly even if you prefer a firmer end result.

Scrambled Eggs with Smoked Salmon

SERVES 4

6 eggs

salt and pepper

4 tablespoons butter

2 tablespoons whipping cream

¼ cup mayonnaise

4 slices of pumpernickel or whole-wheat bread, crusts trimmed

¼ pound thinly sliced smoked salmon

lumpfish or salmon caviar, for garnishing

1 ▲ Season the eggs with salt and pepper. Scramble them using half of the butter. Mix in the cream just before they have finished cooking.

2 Remove from the heat and mix in the mayonnaise. Let cool.

3 Spread the slices of bread with the remaining butter. Cover with smoked salmon, trimming it to fit. Cut in half.

4 Divide the scrambled eggs among the plates, spreading it neatly on the smoked salmon. Top each serving with a heaped tablespoon of caviar.

FRYING EGGS

Short-order cooks know that people have strong feelings about how their eggs should be fried. However they're cooked, fried eggs are natural partners for bacon and other breakfast fare.

1 Heat butter, bacon fat, or oil in a frying pan (to cover the bottom generously) over medium heat. When the fat is sizzling, break each egg and slip it into the pan.

2 ◄ Fry until the egg white is just set and opaque or more firm, according to your taste, 1–1½ minutes. The yolk will still be runny and the base of the egg will be golden brown and crisp. The egg is ready to serve now, for "sunny-side up." Or, for "over easy," gently turn the fried egg over with a slotted spatula, taking care not to break the yolk. Cook until the other side is just browned, 10–15 seconds.

Fried Eggs and Sausage on Tortillas

SERVES 4

½ pound ground pork
½ small onion, minced
1 tablespoon chili powder (or to taste)
½ teaspoon ground cumin
½ teaspoon dried oregano
1 tablespoon vinegar
1 garlic clove, minced
salt and pepper
oil, for frying
4 large corn tortillas
4 eggs
4 tablespoons butter or bacon fat
Mexican hot sauce or salsa, for serving

1 ▲ Put the pork in a bowl and add the onion, spices, oregano, vinegar, garlic, salt, and pepper. Mix well, cover, and refrigerate overnight.

2 ▼ Cook the pork mixture in a large frying pan until it is browned and crumbly, stirring occasionally.

3 Meanwhile, heat 1 inch of oil in a wide saucepan to 365°F. Fry the tortillas until they are crisp and golden brown, keeping them flat. Drain on paper towels and put on a baking sheet. Keep warm in the oven.

4 Fry the eggs in the butter or bacon fat (or use oil for frying if you prefer).

5 Put a tortilla on each plate. Using a slotted spoon, divide the pork mixture among the tortillas. Top each serving with a fried egg. Serve accompanied by hot sauce or salsa.

BAKING EGGS

Baking, or shirring, is one of the simplest ways to cook eggs, yet it produces elegant results. The eggs can be baked individually, in buttered pots (ramekins) or small shallow dishes, or several can be baked in a large dish, on a bed of vegetables, sauce, etc.

Ideas for Baked Eggs

- Coat buttered ramekins with freshly grated Parmesan or pecorino cheese. Dot the eggs with butter and sprinkle each egg very lightly with the Parmesan or pecorino cheese before baking.
- Put a little diced cooked ham, or a few sautéed sliced mushrooms, or crisp croutons, garlic flavored if preferred, in the bottom of each ramekin before breaking in the egg.
- Bake eggs on a bed of creamed spinach, mashed potato or other root vegetables, or puréed broccoli or peas.
- Bake eggs on a bed of tomato sauce and roasted vegetables.
- Bake eggs in hollows made in a cooked stuffing, such as sausage stuffing for chicken or smoked ham and almond stuffing for turkey.
- Bake potatoes, then cut off a lengthwise slice from one side. Scoop out the flesh, leaving a shell ⅛- to ¼-inch thick. Mash the potato with butter, milk, salt, and pepper. Spoon it back into the potato shells and press down firmly. Make a hollow in the top of the mashed potato in each shell and break in an egg. Drizzle a little melted butter over the egg. Bake at 400°F to set the egg white, 5–7 minutes.

1 ▲ **To bake in individual ramekins**: Butter the dishes and sprinkle them with salt and pepper. Break an egg into each, taking care not to pierce the yolk.

3 ▲ Set the dishes in a baking pan. Add enough water to come halfway up the sides of the dishes. Bring to a simmer on top of the stove. Transfer to a preheated 400°F oven. Bake until the whites are just set and the yolks still soft, 5–7 minutes.

2 ▲ Dot the top of each egg with a few small pieces of butter, or add 1 tablespoon of whipping cream to each ramekin.

4 ▲ **To bake on a bed**: Spread a hot savory mixture in a buttered shallow baking dish or in individual ramekins or gratin dishes. Make hollows in the mixture with the back of a spoon. Break an egg into each hollow.

5 ◄ According to recipe directions, dot the eggs with butter, sprinkle with cheese, drizzle with cream, etc. (These toppings help to moisten and flavor the eggs during cooking.) Bake until the whites are just set and the yolks are still soft.

Poaching Eggs

The perfect poached egg has a neat oval shape, a tender white, and a soft yolk. It is unbeatable on a slice of hot buttered toast, or it can be partnered with vegetables (artichoke bottoms, asparagus), seafood (crab, smoked salmon), or meat (ham, bacon, steak) and dressed with a rich sauce. Use the freshest eggs possible because they will be the easiest to poach.

1 First, bring a large, deep pan of water to a boil.

2 ▲ Break each egg and slip it gently into the water. Reduce the heat to low so the water is just simmering. Poach until the eggs are done, 3–4 minutes.

3 ▲ With a slotted spoon, lift out each egg and press it gently; the white should feel just firm but the yolk should still be soft.

The Clotting Factor

If your eggs are more than a few days old, adding white wine vinegar to the poaching water will help the egg white to coagulate, although it will slightly flavor the egg. Use 2 tablespoons vinegar to each quart of water.

4 ◄ If there are any strings of cooked egg white, trim them off with a knife or kitchen scissors. Drain briefly on paper towels. Serve immediately, if wished. Or, warm up the eggs in a bowl of hot water for serving. If the eggs will be served cold, immerse them in a bowl of ice water until needed. Drain the eggs and blot dry gently with paper towels before serving.

Poached Eggs Florentine

Serves 4

1½ pounds spinach leaves, shredded
2 tablespoons butter
3–4 tablespoons whipping cream
⅛ teaspoon grated nutmeg
salt and pepper
4 eggs
1 cup cheese sauce made with Swiss cheese and no mustard
¼ cup shredded Swiss cheese

1 Preheat the broiler.

2 Put the spinach in a large pan with the butter. Cover and cook until the leaves are wilted. Uncover and boil to evaporate the excess liquid.

3 ▲ Mix in the cream, nutmeg, and seasonings. Poach the eggs.

4 Divide the spinach among 4 individual shallow gratin dishes or a large gratin dish. Spread it evenly and make hollows for the eggs. Set a poached egg in each hollow.

5 ▼ Coat the eggs lightly with the cheese sauce. Sprinkle with the shredded cheese. Broil until the cheese has melted and is lightly browned, 2–3 minutes. Serve immediately.

MAKING A ROLLED OR FOLDED OMELET

The versatile rolled or folded omelet can be served plain or filled. There are also flat omelets and soufflé omelets, which may be filled as well. At its simplest, an omelet is made with 2 or 3 eggs, 1–2 teaspoons water, salt, and pepper.

Omelet Fillings

• Add 1 tablespoon minced fresh herbs (a mixture of parsley, chives, and tarragon, for example) to the beaten eggs.

• Scatter 2–3 tablespoons shredded cheese (Swiss, Cheddar) over the omelet before rolling or folding.

• Sauté peeled, seeded, and chopped tomatoes in butter 1–2 minutes. Season with salt and pepper and stir in a little chopped fresh basil. Use to fill the omelet.

• Fill the omelet with thinly sliced strips of prosciutto or cooked ham, or with roasted vegetables, sautéed sliced mushrooms, slow-cooked onions, home-fried potatoes, or buttered asparagus tips.

• Warm leftover pasta (buttered or in sauce); if the shape is long, such as spaghetti, cut it into short pieces. If using buttered pasta, add strips of canned pimiento, sliced black olives, capers, etc. Use to fill the omelet, roll or fold, and sprinkle the top with grated Parmesan cheese.

The Right Pan

Although you can make an omelet in a frying pan or skillet, a special omelet pan, with its curved edge, will make rolling or folding and turning out the omelet easier.

1 ▲ Break the eggs into a bowl and add the water and some salt and pepper. Beat with a fork until just blended but not frothy.

3 ▲ When the butter is foaming and just beginning to turn golden, pour in the egg mixture. Tilt and rotate the pan to spread the eggs in an even layer over the bottom.

5 ▲ With the spatula, loosen the edge of the omelet on one side and tilt the pan so that a third of the omelet rolls over onto itself. (Or, just fold the omelet over in half.)

2 ▲ In an 8-inch omelet pan, melt 1–1½ tablespoons butter over medium-high heat. Tilt and rotate the pan so the bottom and sides are thoroughly coated with butter.

4 ▲ Cook until the omelet starts to set on the base, 5–10 seconds. With a thin spatula, lift the cooked base and tilt the pan so the uncooked egg mixture runs underneath onto the hot pan. Continue cooking in this way until most of the omelet is set but the top is still moist and creamy.

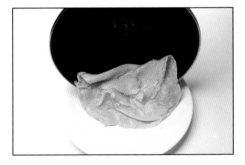

6 ▲ Continue loosening the omelet from its rolled edge, holding the pan over a warmed plate. As the omelet slides out of the pan onto the plate, tilt the pan so the omelet rolls over again on itself into thirds, using the edge of the pan to guide it.

MAKING STIRRED CUSTARD

A homemade stirred custard is a luscious sauce for many hot and cold desserts. It is also the basis for a very rich ice cream, which is essentially a frozen stirred custard enriched with cream.

The secret for success is patience. Don't try to hurry the cooking of the custard by raising the heat.

MAKES ABOUT 2 CUPS

2 cups milk
1 vanilla bean, split in half
4 egg yolks
3–4 tablespoons sugar

Custard Variations
- Use 1 teaspoon vanilla extract instead of the vanilla bean. Omit steps 1 and 2, and add the extract after straining the custard.
- For *Chocolate Custard*: Add 2 ounces semisweet chocolate, grated, to the hot milk and sugar mixture. Stir until smooth before adding to the egg yolks.
- For *Mocha Custard*: Add 2 ounces semisweet chocolate, grated, and 2 teaspoons instant coffee powder or granules.
- For *Orange Custard*: Omit the vanilla bean and instead infuse the milk with the finely pared rind of 1 orange.
- For *Liqueur Custard*: Add 2–3 tablespoons Cognac, kirsch, or other liqueur to the custard.

Damage Repair
If the custard gets too hot and starts to curdle, remove it from the heat immediately and pour it into a bowl. Whisk vigorously until smooth, 2–3 seconds. Then pour it back into the pan and continue cooking.

1 ▲ Put the milk in a heavy-based saucepan. Hold the vanilla bean over the pan and scrape out the tiny black seeds into the milk. Add the split bean to the milk.

3 ▲ In a bowl, lightly beat the egg yolks with the sugar until smoothly blended and creamy. Gradually add the hot milk to the egg yolks, stirring constantly.

5 ▲ Cook, stirring constantly, until the custard thickens to a creamy consistency that coats the spoon, 10–12 minutes. Immediately remove the pan of custard from over the pan of hot water.

2 ▲ Heat the milk until bubbles appear around the edge. Remove from the heat, cover, and set aside to infuse 10 minutes. Remove the split vanilla bean.

4 ▲ Pour the mixture into the top of a double boiler. Set over the bottom pan containing hot water. Put on a medium-low heat, so the water stays below a boil.

6 ▲ Strain the custard into a bowl. If using cold, sprinkle a little superfine sugar over the surface of the custard to help prevent a skin from forming. Set the bowl in a container of ice water and let cool.

MAKING A BATTER

Batters consist mainly of flour, eggs and liquid. They may be thick – for making fritters or coating food to be fried – or thin and pourable, for pancakes, waffles, and crêpes. For a very light result, the eggs can be separated and the whites beaten and folded in.

Pork and Apple Batter Puddings
Make the batter with 4 ounces all-purpose flour, a pinch of salt, 1 egg and 1¼ cups mixed milk and water. The batter can be made in a blender or food processor, but take care not to overmix. Mix together 1 pound ground lean pork, 4 ounces finely chopped or coarsely shredded green apple, 1 small shredded onion, 1 tablespoon chopped fresh parsley, salt and pepper. Shape into 16 small balls. Oil four individual 2½-cup baking dishes and heat in a 425°F oven. Divide the balls among the dishes and bake for 10 minutes. Pour the batter in a pitcher for easy pouring or ladle it from the bowl. Pour the batter over the balls and bake for 35–40 minutes or until risen and golden brown. Serve hot.
Serves 4.

1 ▲ Sift the flour into a bowl along with other dry ingredients such as sugar, baking powder or soda, salt, spices, etc.

2 ▲ Make a well in the center of the dry ingredients and put in the eggs or egg yolks and some of the liquid.

3 ▲ With a wooden spoon, beat together the eggs and liquid in the well just to mix them.

4 ▲ Gradually draw in some of the flour from the sides, stirring vigorously.

5 ▲ When the mixture is smooth, stir in the remaining liquid. The trick is not to overmix – stir just until the ingredients are combined.

6 ▲ If the recipe directs, beat egg whites to a soft peak and fold them into the batter. Do this just before using the batter.

MAKING CRÊPES

These thin, lacy French pancakes are wonderfully versatile. They can be served very simply with just lemon juice and sugar, or turned into more elaborate dishes: folded and warmed in a sauce, rolled around a savory or sweet filling, or stacked in layers like a cake with filling between.

MAKES ABOUT 12

1 cup flour
2 teaspoons sugar (for sweet crêpes)
2 extra large eggs
about 1½ cups milk
2 tablespoons melted butter, plus more for frying (or oil, for frying)

Crêpes with Ricotta and Peaches
Combine 2 cups ricotta cheese, ¼ cup confectioners' sugar, 1 teaspoon vanilla extract, and 2 tablespoons brandy in a bowl. Mix well. Add 4 large, ripe peaches, peeled and diced, and fold in gently. Divide the ricotta and peach mixture among 12 crêpes and spread it evenly over them. Fold each crêpe in half and then in half again, into quarters. Arrange the crêpes in a buttered large oval baking dish, slightly overlapping them. Brush with 2 tablespoons melted butter and sprinkle generously with confectioners' sugar. Bake in a preheated 375°F oven for 10 minutes. Serve the crêpes hot, with raspberry sauce. *Serves 4.*

1 ▲ Make the crêpe batter and let stand at least 20 minutes. Heat an 8-inch crêpe pan over medium heat. The pan is ready for cooking when a few drops of water sprinkled on the surface sizzle immediately. Grease the pan lightly with melted butter or oil. Ladle or pour 3–4 tablespoons batter into the pan. Quickly tilt and rotate the pan so that the batter spreads out to cover the bottom thinly and evenly; pour out any excess batter.

3 ▲ To fill crêpes: For folded crêpes, spread 3–4 tablespoons of filling evenly over each crêpe. Fold in half, then in half again, into quarters. For rolled crêpes, put 3–4 tablespoons of filling near one edge of each crêpe and roll up tightly from that side. To make packages, spoon 3–4 tablespoons of filling in the center of each crêpe. Fold in 2 opposite sides, over the filling, then fold in the other 2 sides. Turn the package over before serving or putting in a baking dish. Filled crêpes are usually baked before serving to heat them through and to brown any topping that may be added.

2 ▲ Cook until the crêpe is set and small holes have appeared, 30–45 seconds. If the cooking seems to be taking too long, increase the heat slightly. Lift the edge of the crêpe with a metal spatula; the base of the crêpe should be lightly brown. Shake the pan vigorously back and forth to loosen the crêpe completely, then turn or flip it over. Cook the other side about 30 seconds. Stack cooked crêpes until ready to fill.

Crêpe-Making Tips
● Crêpe batter should be made at least 20 minutes before using. Refrigerate if holding it longer.
● The batter can be made in a blender or food processor. It must have time to stand before using, as this method incorporates more air.
● Crêpe batter should be the consistency of heavy cream. If it doesn't flow smoothly to make a thin crêpe, add a little more liquid.
● If the batter is lumpy, strain it.
● For best results use a crêpe pan, with a flat bottom and sides that angle straight out without curving.
● Your first crêpe may well be unsuccessful because it will test the consistency of the batter and the temperature of the pan, both of which may need adjusting.
● If more convenient, make crêpes ahead of time. Stack them up as you make them, layered with waxed paper. Let cool completely, then wrap in foil. Refrigerate up to 3 days or freeze for 1 month.

FRUIT & ICES

~

Fruit is a colorful and healthy way to end a meal and this chapter shows how to prepare fruit to achieve a beautiful presentation; to make fruit salads and refreshing iced desserts such as sorbets and ice creams.

PREPARING FRESH FRUIT

PEELING AND TRIMMING FRUIT

Citrus fruit

To peel completely, cut a slice from the top and base. Set the fruit base down on a work surface. Using a small sharp knife, cut off the peel lengthwise in thick strips, taking the colored rind and all the white pith (which has a bitter taste). Cut following the curve of the fruit.

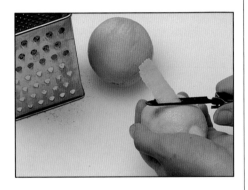

To remove colored rind (or "zest"), use a vegetable peeler to shave off the rind in thick strips, taking none of the white pith. Use these strips whole or cut them into fine shreds with a sharp knife, according to recipe directions. Or, rub the fruit against the fine holes of a metal grater, turning the fruit so you take just the colored rind and not the white pith. Or, use a special tool, called a citrus zester, to take fine threads of rind. (Mince the threads as an alternative to grating.)

Kiwi fruit

Follow citrus fruit technique, taking off the peel thinly in lengthwise strips.

Apples, pears, quinces, mangoes, papayas

Use a small sharp knife or a vegetable peeler. Take off the peel in long strips, as thinly as possible.

Peaches, apricots

Cut a cross in the base. Immerse the fruit in boiling water. Leave 10–30 seconds (according to ripeness), then drain and immerse in ice water. The skin should slip off easily.

Pineapple

Cut off the leafy crown. Cut a slice from the base and set the pineapple upright. With a sharp knife, cut off the peel lengthwise, cutting thickly to remove the brown "eyes" with it.

Bananas, litchis, avocado

Make a small cut and remove the peel with your fingers.

Passion fruit, pomegranates

Cut in half, or cut a slice off the top. With a spoon, scoop the flesh and seeds into a bowl.

Star fruit (carambola)

Trim off the tough, darkened edges of the five segments.

Rhubarb

Cut off the leaves and discard them (they are poisonous). Peel off any tough skin.

Fresh currants (red, black, white)

Pull through the tines of a fork to remove the currants from the stem.

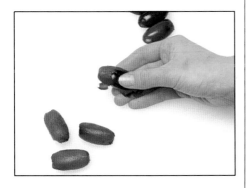

Fresh dates

Squeeze gently at the stem end to remove the rather tough skin.

CORING AND PITTING OR SEEDING FRUIT

Apples, pears, quinces

For whole fruit, use an apple corer to stamp out the whole core from stem end to base. Alternatively, working up from the base, use a melon baller to cut out the core. Leave the stem end intact.

For halves, use a melon baller to scoop out the core. Cut out the stem and base with a small sharp knife.
For quarters, cut out the stem and core with a serrated knife.

Citrus fruit

With the tip of a pointed knife, nick out seeds from slices or sections.

Cherries

Use a cherry pitter for the neatest results.

Peaches, apricots, nectarines, plums

Cut the fruit in half, cutting around the indentation. Twist the halves apart. Lift out the pit, or lever it out with the tip of a sharp knife.

Fresh dates

Cut the fruit lengthwise in half and lift out the pit. Or, if the fruit is to be used whole, cut in from the stem end with a thin-bladed knife to loosen the pit, then remove it.

Mangoes

Cut lengthwise on either side of the large flat seed in the center. Curve the cut slightly to follow the shape of the seed. Also, cut the flesh from the two thin ends of the seed.

Papayas, melons

Cut the fruit in half. Scoop out the seeds from the central hollow, then scrape away any fibers.

Pineapple

For spears and wedges, cut out the core neatly with a sharp knife.

For rings, cut out the core with a small cookie cutter.

Grapes

Cut the fruit lengthwise in half. Use a small knife to nick out the seeds. Alternatively, use the curved end of a sterilized bobby pin.

Gooseberries

Use scissors to trim off the stem and flower ends.

Star fruit (carambola), watermelon

With the tip of a pointed knife, nick out seeds from slices.

Strawberries

Use a special huller to remove leafy green top and central core. Or, cut these out with a small sharp knife.

Avocado

Cut the fruit in half lengthwise. Stick the tip of a sharp knife into the seed and lever it out without damaging the surrounding flesh.

CUTTING FRUIT

Apples, quinces

For rings, remove the core and seeds with an apple corer. Set the fruit on its side and cut across into thick or thin rings, as required.

For slices, cut the fruit in half and remove core and seeds with a melon baller. Set one half cut-side down and

cut it across into neat slices, thick or thin according to recipe directions. Or, cut the fruit into quarters and remove core and seeds with a knife. Cut lengthwise into neat slices.

Pears

For "fans," cut the fruit in half and remove core and seeds with a melon baller. Set one half cut-side down and cut lengthwise into thin slices, not cutting all the way through at the stem end. Gently fan out the slices so they are overlapping each other evenly. Transfer the pear fan to plate or pastry shell using a metal spatula.

For slices, follow apple technique.

Keeping Fresh Color

If exposed to the air for long, the cut flesh of some fruits and vegetables starts to turn brown. Those that tend to brown include apples, bananas, peaches, and avocado. So if prepared fruit has to wait before being served or cooked, sprinkle the cut surfaces with lemon juice. Or, you can immerse hard fruits in water and lemon juice, but do not soak or the fruit may become soggy.

Citrus fruit
For slices, using a serrated knife, cut the fruit across into neat slices.

For sections, hold the peeled fruit in your cupped palm, over a bowl to catch the juice. Working from the side of the fruit to the center, slide the knife down one side of a separating membrane to free the flesh from it. Then slide the knife down the other side of that section to free it from the membrane there. Drop the section into the bowl. Continue cutting out the sections, folding back the membrane like the pages of a book as you work. When all the sections have been cut out, squeeze all the juice from the membrane.

Peaches, nectarines, apricots, plums
For slices, follow apple technique.

Papayas, avocado
For slices, follow apple technique. Or, cut the unpeeled fruit into wedges, removing the central seeds or seed. Set each wedge peel side down and slide the knife down the length to cut the flesh away from the peel.
For fans, follow pear technique.

Melon
For slices, follow papaya technique.
For balls, use a melon baller.

Mangoes
Cut the peeled flesh into slices or cubes, according to recipe directions.

Bananas Baked with Rum
Quarter 4 bananas and put in a small baking dish. Sprinkle with a mixture of ¼ cup melted butter, 3 tablespoons light brown sugar, 1–2 tablespoons lemon juice, and 6 tablespoons light rum or orange juice. Turn to coat the pieces. Bake at 400°F for 20 minutes, basting occasionally. Serve hot. *Serves 4.*

Pineapple
For spears, cut the peeled fruit lengthwise in half and then into quarters. Cut each quarter into spears and cut out the core.
For chunks, cut the peeled fruit into spears. Remove the core. Cut across each spear into chunks.
For rings, cut the peeled fruit across into slices. Stamp out the central core from each slice using a cookie cutter.

Kiwi fruit, Star fruit (carambola)
Cut the fruit across into neat slices; discard the ends.

Banana
Cut the fruit across into neat slices. Or, cut in half and then lengthwise into quarters.

PREPARING MELON

Melons make attractive containers for salads, both sweet and savory. Small melons can be used for individual servings, while large watermelons will hold salads to serve a crowd, providing a festive centerpiece at the same time!

Special tools, such as melon cutters with V- and U-shaped blades, and melon ballers, make decorative preparation easier.

1 ◄ For a plain edge: Cut the melon in half and scoop out the central seeds. Remove most of the flesh with a melon baller. Or, cut it out with a grapefruit knife or scoop it out with a large spoon. Reserve the flesh for the salad. Continue scraping out the flesh, to leave an even, usually thin, layer.

2 ▲ For a zigzag edge: First cut a line around the circumference of the melon to ensure that your finished edge will be straight. Using a sharp knife, insert it on the cut line at an angle. Continue making an angled cut about ½- to 2-inches long, according to the size of the melon. Cut all the way to the center of the melon. Remove the knife.

3 ▲ Insert the knife at the top of the angled cut and cut back down to the line at a right angle to the first cut, forming a V. Continue cutting V-shapes in this way all around the melon. If available, a special melon cutter with a V-shaped blade will make the job easier.

4 ▲ Lift the melon halves apart. Remove the seeds and scoop out the flesh as above.

Citrus Garnishes
The technique for preparing melons can also be used for lemons and oranges. These make attractive containers for cold and iced desserts. Another idea: Cut a lemon in half with a zigzag edge, but don't hollow out the halves. Instead, trim the base of each so it will sit flat, then dip the points of the V's in minced parsley. Serve these lemon halves instead of wedges with fish.

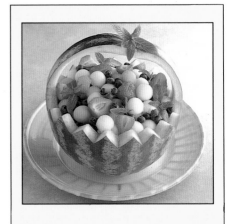

5 ▲ For a scalloped edge: You can do this freehand following the technique for cutting a zigzag edge, but instead cutting curves. However, it is much easier, and the results are better, if you use a special melon cutter with a U-shaped blade.

Watermelon Basket
Cut a watermelon basket as directed above. Scoop out the flesh with a melon baller and nick out as many of the black seeds as you can. Mix the watermelon balls with balls of cantaloupe and honeydew melon, blueberries, and strawberries. Pile the fruit back in the watermelon basket for serving.

6 ▲ For a melon basket: Cut a plain, zigzag, or scalloped edge, starting just off center. Cut around the melon to a point opposite where you started.

7 ▲ Cut up over the top of the melon and down to the point you began. Lift off the freed wedge of melon. Repeat on the other end.

8 ▲ Cut out the flesh from under the "handle." Cut or scoop the flesh from the melon as before.

Melon Salad with Herbs

SERVES 4 AS A FIRST COURSE

2 small cantaloupe melons
½ honeydew melon
½ hothouse cucumber
1 cup small cherry tomatoes
1½ tablespoons minced fresh parsley
1 tablespoon snipped fresh chives
1 tablespoon chopped fresh mint
FOR THE DRESSING
6 tablespoons salad oil
2 tablespoons red wine vinegar
1 teaspoon sugar
salt and pepper

1 Cut the cantaloupes in half, with a plain, zigzag, or scalloped edge. Scoop out the seeds and central fibers. Using a melon baller, take small balls of flesh and put them in a bowl. Scrape some of the remaining flesh from the melon halves. Set the melon shells aside.

2 Remove seeds and fibers from the honeydew melon. Scoop out the flesh in small balls and add to the cantaloupe balls.

3 ▲ Use the melon baller to make balls of cucumber, or cut into cubes.

4 Add the cucumber to the melon balls with the cherry tomatoes.

5 For the dressing, combine the ingredients in a screwtop jar and shake well. Add the dressing to the bowl and toss together. Cover and refrigerate the salad 2–3 hours.

6 Just before serving, stir in the herbs. Divide the salad among the melon shells, with all the juice.

PREPARING FRESH PINEAPPLE

Pineapple can be prepared in many decorative ways, apart from rings, spears, and cubes.

1 ▲ For a pineapple boat: Trim off any browned ends from the green leaves of the crown. Trim the stem end if necessary. With a long sharp knife, cut the pineapple lengthwise in half, through the crown.

2 ▲ Cut a thin slice from the base of each half so it has a flat surface and will not rock.

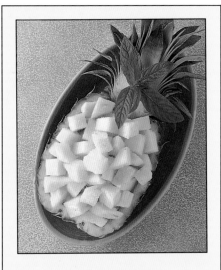

Spiked Pineapple Boat
Cut 2 small to medium-sized pineapples in half and scoop out the flesh. Cut the pineapple flesh into neat, small pieces. Put them back in the pineapple halves. Sprinkle each half with 1–2 tablespoons rum, kirsch, apricot brandy, or Grand Marnier. If desired, sprinkle with a little sugar to taste. Toss the fruit to mix the liquor and sugar evenly. Cover tightly and chill 20–30 minutes before serving. *Serves 4.*

3 ▲ With a small sharp knife, cut straight across the top and bottom of the central core in each half. Then cut lengthwise at a slant on either side of the core. This will cut out the core in a V-shape.

4 ▲ With a curved serrated grapefruit knife, cut out the flesh from each half. The boats are now ready for filling with a salad, a dessert, or with ice cream, fruit ice, or sorbet.

5 ▲ For pineapple wedges: Trim the crown and base as above. Cut the fruit lengthwise in half, through the crown, and then into quarters.

6 ▲ Cut the central core from each quarter. Slide the knife under the flesh to loosen it from the peel, but leave it in place.

7 ▲ Cut across the flesh on each wedge. Pull out the slices slightly in alternate directions. If desired, sprinkle the fruit lightly with sugar before serving.

MAKING SORBETS AND FRUIT ICES

Sorbets and fruit ices are most refreshing desserts. A fruit ice is made by freezing a sweetened fruit purée, whereas a sorbet is made from fruit juice or purée mixed with a sugar syrup. In addition, there are sorbets based on wine or liqueur. The Italian "granita" uses the same mixture as a sorbet, but it is stirred during freezing to give it its characteristic coarse texture. A sherbet normally contains milk or cream.

Strawberry Ice
Purée 1½ pints strawberries with ½ cup sugar and ½ cup orange juice in a blender or food processor. Be sure the sugar has dissolved completely. Add 1 tablespoon lemon juice. Taste the mixture and add more sugar or orange or lemon juice, if required. (The mixture should be well flavored.) Chill, then transfer to an ice cream machine and freeze until firm. *Makes about 2½ cups.*

Variations
• Use raspberries or blackberries instead of strawberries.
• Use 4 cups peeled, sliced, and pitted peaches or nectarines instead of strawberries.
• Add 1–2 tablespoons of fruit liqueur (to match the fruit used).

1 ▲ For a fruit ice: Prepare the fruit, removing peel, pits, hulls, stems, etc. Purée the fruit with sugar and liquid in a blender or food processor until very smooth. Be sure that the sugar has dissolved completely.

3 ▲ For a sorbet: If using citrus fruit, peel off strips of rind. Squeeze the juice from the fruit. Alternatively, purée fruit in a blender or food processor (first cooking if necessary).

5 ▲ Stir in the fruit juice or purée. Strain the mixture into a bowl, if necessary, and chill well. Then transfer the mixture to an ice cream machine and freeze following the manufacturer's instructions.

2 ▲ Add additional flavorings as directed in the recipe (alcohol, herbs, for example). If using berries with seeds (raspberries, blackberries, etc.), press the purée through a fine-mesh nylon strainer. Chill the purée well. Then transfer to an ice cream machine and freeze following manufacturer's instructions.

4 ▲ Put the strips of rind (or other flavorings such as vanilla bean, spices) in a saucepan with sugar and water and bring to a boil, stirring to dissolve the sugar. Let cool.

Still-Freezing Fruit Ice
If you don't have an ice cream machine, you can "still-freeze" the fruit ice or sorbet in the freezer. Pour it into a metal pan or tray, cover, and freeze until set around the edge. Turn it into a bowl and break it into small pieces. Beat with an electric mixer or in a food processor until slushy. Return to the metal pan and freeze again until set around the edge. Repeat the beating once or twice more, then let freeze until firm.

MAKING A BERRY SAUCE

A smooth, uncooked berry sauce, called a "coulis" in French, has a refreshing flavor and beautiful color. According to how much sugar you add, a berry sauce can be a sweet complement or tart contrast to cake, pastry, ice cream, or a fruit dessert.

You can use fresh or frozen berries for the sauce. If using frozen berries, partially thaw them and drain on paper towels before puréeing.

MAKES ABOUT 1 CUP

1 pint berries (raspberries, strawberries, blackberries, boysenberries, etc.)

¼–½ cup confectioners' sugar

squeeze of lemon juice (optional)

1–2 tablespoons kirsch or fruit liqueur (optional)

1 ▲ Hull the berries if necessary. Put them in a bowl of cold water and swirl them around briefly. Scoop out and spread on paper towels. Pat dry. Purée the berries in a blender or food processor. Turn the machine on and off a few times and scrape down the bowl to be sure all the berries are evenly puréed.

2 ▲ For raspberries, blackberries, and other berries with small seeds, press the purée through a fine-mesh nylon strainer. Add confectioners' sugar to taste, plus a little lemon juice and/or liqueur – framboise – if desired (for example, raspberry liqueur for a raspberry sauce). Stir well to dissolve the sugar completely.

Iced Macaroon Cream with Raspberry Sauce

SERVES 6–8

3 cups whipping cream

¼ cup brandy

2 tablespoons sugar

12 crisp almond macaroons (about 4 ounces), coarsely crushed

raspberries, for decorating

1 cup raspberry sauce, for serving

1 ▲ Put the cream in a large bowl, preferably chilled, and whip until it starts to thicken.

2 Add the brandy and sugar. Continue whipping until the cream will hold stiff peaks.

3 ▼ Add the macaroons and fold evenly into the cream.

~ **VARIATIONS** ~

Use coarsely broken meringue nests instead of macaroons. Use orange juice instead of brandy.

4 Spoon into 6 1-cup or 8 ¾-cup ramekins, or a 1½-quart smooth-sided mold. Press in evenly to be sure there are no air pockets. Smooth the surface. Cover and freeze until firm. (Do not freeze more than 1 day.)

5 ▼ To serve, dip the molds in hot water for 5–10 seconds, then invert onto a serving plate. Lift off the molds. Refrigerate the desserts 15–20 minutes, to soften slightly.

6 Decorate with raspberries and serve with the raspberry sauce.

BREADS & CAKES

~

There is nothing quite so satisfying as the aroma of freshly-baked bread. Even if you're a beginner, you'll find the methods for quick breads, yeast breads and cake making techniques easy to follow.

MAKING QUICK BREADS AND MUFFINS

As their name denotes, these breads are fast and easy to make. The leavening agent reacts quickly with moisture and heat to make the breads and muffins rise, without the need for a rising period before baking.

The leavening agent is usually baking soda or baking powder, which is a mixture of baking soda and an acid salt such as cream of tartar. It will start to work as soon as it comes into contact with liquid, so don't mix the dry and liquid ingredients until just before you are ready to fill the muffin cups and bake.

In addition to the thick-batter quick breads discussed here, there are also thin-batter quick breads such as pancakes and waffles, and quick breads that are made from soft doughs such as biscuits.

1 ▲ **For muffins**: Combine the dry ingredients in a bowl. It is a good idea to sift the flour with the leavening agent, salt, and any spices to mix them. Add the liquid ingredients and stir just until the dry ingredients are moistened; the batter will not be smooth. Do not overmix in an attempt to remove all the lumps. If you do, the muffins will not be tender and will have tunnels in them.

2 ▲ Divide the batter evenly among the greased muffin cups (or line the cups with paper cupcake liners), filling them about two-thirds full. Bake until golden brown and a wooden skewer inserted in the center comes out clean. To prevent soggy bottoms, remove the muffins immediately from the cups to a wire rack. Let cool, and serve warm or at room temperature.

Granola Muffins
Make the batter from 1 cup flour, 2½ teaspoons baking powder, 2 tablespoons sugar, 1 cup milk, ¼ cup melted butter or corn oil, and 1 egg, adding 1¾ cups granola-type cereal with raisins to the dry ingredients. Pour into muffins cups (2½- to 2¾-inch diameter, 1½-inches deep). Bake in a preheated 400°F oven until golden brown, about 20 minutes. *Makes 10.*

3 ▲ **For fruit and/or nut breads**: Method 1: Stir together all the liquid ingredients. Add the dry ingredients and beat just until smoothly blended. Method 2: Beat the butter with the sugar until the mixture is light and fluffy. Beat in the eggs followed by the other liquid ingredients. Stir in the dry ingredients. Pour the batter into a prepared pan (typically a loaf pan). Bake until a wooden skewer inserted in the center comes out clean. If the bread is browning too quickly, cover the top with foil.

4 ▲ Cool in the pan 5 minutes, then unmold onto a wire rack to cool completely. A lengthwise crack on the surface is characteristic of quick breads. For easier slicing, wrap the bread in wax paper and overwrap in foil, then store overnight at room temperature.

Banana Bread

MAKES 1 LOAF

1½ cups flour
2¼ teaspoons baking powder
½ teaspoon salt
¾ teaspoon ground cinnamon (optional)
¼ cup wheat germ
5 tablespoons butter, at room temperature, or ⅓ cup shortening
⅔ cup sugar
¾ teaspoon grated lemon rind
1¼ cups mashed ripe bananas (2–3 bananas)
2 eggs, beaten to mix

1 Preheat the oven to 350°F. Grease and flour an 8½- × 4½-inch loaf pan.

2 ▲ Sift the flour, baking powder, salt, and cinnamon, if using, into a bowl. Stir in the wheat germ.

3 ▲ In another bowl, beat the butter or shortening with the sugar and lemon rind until the mixture is light and fluffy.

4 ▲ Add the mashed bananas and eggs and mix well.

5 Add the dry ingredients and blend quickly and evenly.

~ **VARIATION** ~

For Banana Walnut Bread, add ½–¾ cup finely chopped walnuts with the dry ingredients.

6 ▼ Spoon into the prepared loaf pan. Bake until a wooden skewer inserted in the center comes out clean, about 1 hour.

7 Let the bread cool in the pan about 5 minutes, then unmould onto a wire rack to cool completely.

MAKING YEAST DOUGH

Making bread is a very enjoyable and satisfying culinary experience – with no other preparation do you have such "hands-on" contact. From the kneading through to the shaping of the risen dough, you are working with a living organism, yeast, not a chemical leavening agent. Yeast is available either dry or fresh. Active dry yeast keeps longer. Compressed fresh yeast should be refrigerated.

Everyday White Bread
Mix 2 packages active dry yeast with ⅓ cup warm water; add 1 teaspoon sugar. Sift 5½ cups flour into a large bowl with ½ table-spoon salt and 1 tablespoon sugar. Make a well in the center and add the yeast mixture, 1 cup warm milk, ¾ cup warm water, and 2 tablespoons melted and cooled butter. Mix to a soft dough, adding more flour if necessary, then knead until smooth and elastic. Let rise until doubled in bulk. Punch the dough to deflate it. Divide it in half and shape each piece into a loaf, tucking the ends under. Put in 2 greased 8½- × 4½-inch loaf pans. Leave in a warm place to rise, 30–45 minutes. If desired, lightly beat 1 egg with 1 tablespoon milk and glaze the tops of the loaves. Bake in a preheated 450°F oven 35–40 minutes. *Makes 2 loaves.*

1 ▲ Put the yeast in a small bowl and add some of the warm liquid (105–110°F) called for in the recipe. Let dry yeast soak for 1 minute, then whisk to dissolve; mash fresh yeast to blend. Add a little sugar if the recipe directs.

2 ▲ Sift the flour into a large warm bowl (with other dry ingredients such as salt). Make a well in the center and add the yeast mixture plus any other liquid ingredients.

3 ▲ Using your fingers or a spoon, gradually draw the flour into the liquids. Continue until all the flour is incorporated and the dough pulls away from the sides of the bowl. If the dough feels too soft and wet, work in a little more flour. If it will not come together, add a little more liquid.

4 ▲ Turn the dough onto a lightly floured surface. Fold the dough over onto itself toward you, and then press it down away from you with the heels of your hands. Rotate the dough slightly and fold and press it again. Knead until the dough looks satiny and feels elastic, about 10 minutes.

5 ▲ Shape the dough into a ball. Put it in a lightly greased bowl and rotate the dough so that the surface is lightly greased all over. Cover the bowl with a towel or plastic wrap. Set it aside in a warm, draft-free place (about 80°F).

6 ▲ Let the dough rise until it is doubled in bulk, 1–1½ hours. To test if it is sufficiently risen, press a finger about 1 inch into the dough and withdraw it quickly: the indentation should remain.

7 ▲ Gently punch the center of the dough with your fist to deflate it and fold the edges to the center. Turn the dough onto a lightly floured surface and knead it again for 2–3 minutes. If the recipe directs, shape it into a ball again and let rise a second time.

8 ▲ Shape the dough into loaves, rolls, or other shapes as directed. Put into prepared pans or onto baking sheets. Cover and let rise in a warm place again, ¾–1 hour. If the recipe directs, glaze the loaves or rolls before baking.

9 ◄ Bake in the center of a preheated oven until well risen and golden brown. To test for doneness, turn out of the pan and tap the base with your knuckle. If it sounds hollow, it is fully cooked. Immediately transfer to a wire rack for cooling.

SHAPING ROLLS

A basket of freshly baked rolls, in decorative shapes, is a delightful accompaniment for soups or salads. After shaping, arrange the rolls on a baking sheet, leaving space around each roll for spreading, and let rise for 30 minutes before baking.

Working with Yeast
- A ¼-ounce package of active dry yeast contains 1 tablespoon. One cake of compressed fresh yeast is equivalent to a package of dry yeast. For quick-rising dry yeast, combine it with the flour and other dry ingredients, then add the liquids (which should be warmer than for ordinary active dry yeast). Or, follow recipe directions.
- If you are in any doubt about the freshness of the yeast, it is a good idea to "proof" it: set the yeast mixture in a warm place. After 5–10 minutes, the mixture should be foamy. If it isn't, discard it and start again.

1 ▲ For Parker House rolls: Roll out the risen dough to ¼-inch thickness and cut out 2½- to 3-inch rounds, using a floured cutter. Brush the rounds with melted butter. Fold them in half, slightly off-center so the top overlaps the bottom. Press the folded edge firmly. Arrange on a greased baking sheet.

2 ▲ For butterhorn rolls: Roll out the risen dough to a large round about ¼-inch thick. Brush with melted butter. With a sharp knife, cut into wedges that are 2½–3 inches at their wide end. Roll up each wedge, from the wide end. Set the rolls on a greased baking sheet, placing the points underneath.

3 ◄ For bowknot rolls: Divide the risen dough into pieces. Roll each with your palms on a lightly floured surface to make ropes that are about ½-inch thick. Divide the ropes into 9-inch lengths. Tie each length of dough loosely into a knot, tucking the ends under. Arrange the rolls on a greased baking sheet.

MAKING A BUTTER CAKE

The butter cake, with its tender crumb and rich, moist flavor, is always popular. It is delicious enough to be served plain, with just a dusting of sugar (as with pound cake), or it can be layered and frosted.

To make a butter cake, the fat and sugar are "creamed" together before the eggs and dry ingredients are added. The fat (butter, margarine, or shortening) should be soft enough to be beaten, so if necessary remove it from the refrigerator and let it stand at room temperature at least 30 minutes. For best results, the eggs should be at room temperature, too.

Mocha Spongecake
Make the mixture using 6 ounces each butter or margarine, sugar and self-rising flour and 3 eggs. Divide between two mixing bowls. To one add 1 tablespoon strong black coffee; to the other add 1 tablespoon cocoa powder mixed to a paste with 1–2 tablespoons boiling water. Place alternate spoonfuls of each flavor, side by side, in two greased and baselined 7-inch round layer cake pans. Smooth the top with a spatula. Bake at 350°F for 25–30 minutes. Turn out on to a wire rack and let cool. Sandwich the cakes together with coffee butter frosting. Cover the top, or both top and sides, with the coffee or chocolate butter frosting.

1 ▲ Sift the flour with the salt, leavening agent(s), and any other dry ingredients, such as spices or cocoa powder. Set aside.

2 ▲ Put the fat in a large, deep bowl and beat with an electric mixer at medium speed until the texture is soft and pliable.

3 ▲ Add the sugar to the creamed fat gradually. With the mixer at medium-high speed, beat it into the fat until the mixture is pale and very fluffy, 4–5 minutes. The sugar should be completely incorporated. During this process, air will be beaten into the mixture, which will help the cake to rise.

4 ▲ Add the eggs or egg yolks, one at a time, beating well after each addition (about 45 seconds). Scrape the bowl often so all the ingredients are evenly combined. When adding the eggs, the mixture may begin to curdle, especially if the eggs are cold. If this happens, add 1 tablespoon of the measured flour.

5 ▲ Add the dry ingredients to the beaten mixture, beating at low speed just until smoothly combined.

6 ▲ If the recipe calls for any liquid, add it in small portions alternately with portions of the dry ingredients.

7 ▲ If the recipe directs, beat egg whites separately until frothy, add sugar, and continue beating until stiff peaks form. Fold into the batter.

8 ▲ Pour the batter into a cake pan or pans, prepared according to recipe directions, and bake as directed.

9 ▲ To test butter cakes for doneness, insert a cake tester, skewer, or wooden toothpick into the center; it should come out clean.

MAKING SEVEN-MINUTE FROSTING

This fluffy white frosting has an attractive gloss and a texture like divinity candy. It is ideal for filling and frosting layer cakes.

MAKES ENOUGH TO FROST THE TOP AND SIDES OF TWO 9-INCH CAKE LAYERS

1½ cups sugar
¼ teaspoon cream of tartar
2 egg whites
¼ cup cold water
1 tablespoon light corn syrup
2 teaspoons vanilla extract

1 ▲ Combine the sugar, cream of tartar, egg whites, water, and corn syrup in a large heatproof bowl or large double boiler. Stir just to mix.

2 ▲ Set the bowl over a saucepan of boiling water. The base of the bowl should not touch the water.

Seven-Minute Frosting Variations
• For *Orange Frosting*: Use orange juice instead of water and add 1 teaspoon grated orange rind. Reduce the vanilla to ½ teaspoon.
• For *Lemon Frosting*: Use 2 tablespoons each lemon juice and water and add ½ teaspoon grated lemon rind. Reduce the vanilla to ½ teaspoon.

---

3 ▲ Beat with a handheld electric mixer at high speed until the frosting is thick and white, and will form stiff peaks, about 7 minutes.

4 ▲ Remove from the heat. Add the vanilla and continue beating until the frosting has cooled slightly, about 3 minutes. Use immediately.

MAKING A ONE-BOWL CAKE

Many cakes are made by an easy "one-bowl" method where all the ingredients are combined in a bowl and beaten thoroughly. The mixture can also be made in a food processor, but take care not to overprocess.

Chiffon cakes are a variation on this theme. The eggs are separated and the batter is made by the one-bowl method using the yolks. The whites are beaten separately and then folded into the batter.

1 ▲ Sift the dry ingredients (flour, salt, leavening agents, spices, and so on) into a bowl.

2 ▲ Add the liquid ingredients (eggs, melted fat, milk, fruit juices, and so on) and beat until smooth, with an electric mixer for speed. Pour the batter into the prepared pans and bake as directed.

MAKING BUTTER FROSTING

Simple to make and easy to spread, butter frosting is ideal for butter cakes, layer cakes, and spongecakes. The basic vanilla frosting can be varied with many other flavors, and it can be tinted with food coloring, too.

MAKES ENOUGH TO FROST THE TOP AND SIDES OF TWO 9-INCH CAKE LAYERS

9 tablespoons butter, preferably unsalted, at room temperature

3 cups confectioners' sugar, sifted

1½ teaspoons vanilla extract

about 2 tablespoons milk

1 ▲ Put the butter in a deep mixing bowl and beat it with an electric mixer at medium speed, or a wooden spoon, until it is soft and pliable.

2 ▲ Gradually add the confectioners' sugar, and beat at medium-high speed. Continue beating until the mixture is pale and fluffy.

3 ▲ Add the vanilla extract and 1 tablespoon milk. Beat until smooth and of a spreading consistency. If it is too thick, beat in more milk. If too thin, beat in more sugar.

Butter Frosting Variations
● For *Orange or Lemon Butter Frosting*: Grate the rind from 1 small orange or ½ lemon; squeeze the juice. Beat in the rind with the sugar; use juice instead of the vanilla and milk.
● For *Chocolate Butter Frosting*: Add 6 tablespoons unsweetened cocoa powder, beating it in with the sugar. Increase milk to 3–4 tablespoons.

● For *Mocha Butter Frosting*: Warm the milk and dissolve 1 tablespoon instant coffee powder in it; cool and use to make chocolate butter frosting, adding more milk if needed.
● For *Coffee Butter Frosting*: Warm the milk and dissolve 1½ tablespoons of instant coffee powder in it; cool before adding to the butter frosting.

German Chocolate Cupcakes

MAKES 24

4 ounces sweet cooking chocolate, cut into small pieces

¼ cup water

2 cups cake flour

1 teaspoon baking powder

½ teaspoon baking soda

pinch of salt

1½ cups sugar

¾ cup butter or shortening, at room temperature

⅔ cup buttermilk or milk

1 teaspoon vanilla extract

3 eggs

1 recipe quantity butter frosting, flavored to taste

1 Preheat the oven to 350°F. Grease and flour 24 muffin pans, 2½ to 2¾ inches in diameter, or line them with paper cupcake liners.

2 ▲ Put the chocolate and water in a bowl set over a pan of almost simmering water. Heat until melted and smooth, stirring. Remove from the heat and let cool.

3 Sift the flour, baking powder, soda, salt, and sugar into a large bowl. Add the chocolate mixture, butter, buttermilk, and vanilla.

4 ▲ With an electric mixer on medium-low speed, beat until smoothly blended. Increase the speed to high and beat 2 minutes. Add the eggs and beat 2 minutes.

5 Divide the batter evenly among the muffin pans.

6 Bake until a toothpick inserted into the center of a cupcake comes out clean, 20–25 minutes. Cool in the pans 10 minutes, then unmold and let cool completely on a wire rack.

7 ▼ Frost the top of each cupcake with butter frosting, swirling it into a peak in the center.

PREPARING CAKE PANS

Instructions vary from recipe to recipe for preparing cake pans. Some are simply greased, some are greased and floured, some are lined with paper. There are some (such as for angel food cakes) that are not greased at all. The preparation required is based on the type of cake batter and the length of the baking time.

Flavorful Coatings

Some cake recipes direct that the greased pan be coated with sugar, cocoa powder, or fine crumbs. Follow the method for flouring.

1 ▲ To grease a pan: Use butter, shortening, oil, or vegetable cooking spray. If using butter or shortening, hold a small piece in a paper towel (or use your fingers), and rub it all over the bottom and up the side of the pan to make a thin, even coating. If using oil, brush it on with a pastry brush.

2 ▲ To flour a pan: Put a small scoopful of flour in the center of the greased pan. Tip and rotate the pan so that the flour spreads and coats all over the bottom and up the side. Turn the pan over and shake out excess flour, tapping the base of the pan to dislodge any pockets of flour.

3 ▲ To line the bottom of a pan: Use wax or parchment paper. Set the pan on the paper and draw around the base. Cut out this circle, square, or rectangle, cutting just inside the drawn line. Press the paper circle smoothly onto the bottom of the pan.

4 ▲ To line the sides of a pan: Cut a strip of wax or parchment paper long enough to wrap around the outside of the pan and overlap by 1½ inches. The strip should be wide enough to extend 1 inch above the rim of the cake pan.

5 ▲ Fold the strip lengthwise at the 1-inch point and crease it firmly. With scissors, snip at regular intervals along the 1-inch fold, from the edge to the crease. Line the side of the pan, putting the snipped part of the strip on the bottom of the pan.

6 ▲ For square and rectangular cake pans, fold the paper and crease it with your fingernail to fit snugly into the corners of the pan. Then press the bottom paper lining into place.

7 ▲ If the recipe directs, grease the paper before you put it in the pan. If the pan is to be floured, do this after the paper is in place.

8 ▲ To line muffin cups: Use paper cupcake liners of the required size. Or grease and flour the cups.

9 ▲ To line a jelly-roll pan: Cut a rectangle of wax or parchment paper 2 inches larger all around than the pan. Grease the bottom of the pan lightly to prevent the paper slipping.

10 ▲ Lay the paper evenly in the pan. With the a table knife, press the paper into the angle all around the bottom of the pan, creasing the paper firmly but not cutting it.

11 ▲ With scissors, snip the paper in the corners, from top to bottom, so it will fit neatly into them. Grease the paper according to recipe directions, unless using nonstick silicone paper.

MAKING A SPONGECAKE WITH SEPARATED EGGS

This version of spongecake is easier to make than the classic spongecake that uses whole eggs, but the results are no less tender and delicious. There is no need to set the bowl over a pan of simmering water for beating, although if you are using a hand whisk, rather than an electric mixer or rotary beater, you may want to do so to speed up the thickening of the egg yolk and sugar mixture and to increase its volume. Bowls and beaters used with egg whites must be scrupulously clean and greasefree.

1 ▲ Separate the eggs, taking care that there is no trace of yolk with the whites. Put the yolks and whites in separate large bowls.

2 ▲ Add most of the sugar to the yolks. With a handheld or countertop electric mixer, beat at medium-high speed until the mixture is very thick and pale. Lift out the beaters. The mixture on the beaters should trail back onto the surface of the remaining mixture in the bowl to make a ribbon that holds its shape.

3 ▲ Beat the egg whites until they form soft peaks (if not using a copper bowl, add a pinch of cream of tartar once the whites become frothy). Add the remaining sugar and beat until the whites will form stiff peaks.

4 ▲ With a rubber spatula, fold the sifted flour into the egg-yolk mixture, then fold in the beaten egg whites. Fold gently but thoroughly. Pour the batter into the prepared pan or pans and bake as directed.

A Butter Spongecake
This whisked sponge, made with whole or separated eggs, is more rich and trickier to make, as melted butter is folded in just before pouring into the pan.

Making a Classic Spongecake

The classic spongecake contains no fat and no leavening agents – just eggs, sugar, and flour. The light, airy texture of the finished cake depends on the air beaten into the batter.

Sometimes the eggs are separated for a spongecake and sometimes the cake is enriched with butter (called a "genoise", or butter spongecake).

Spongecake can be simply dusted with confectioners' sugar, layered with sweetened whipped cream, filled with preserves or fruit if desired, or used to make a jelly roll.

If you use a countertop electric mixer to beat the eggs and sugar, or if using separated eggs, there is no need to set the bowl over a pan of simmering water.

Basic Spongecake
Make the cake batter using 4 whole eggs, ¾ cup sugar, and ¾ cup cake flour. Pour the batter into a greased, bottom-lined, and floured 9-inch round cake pan. Bake in a preheated 350°F oven 30–35 minutes. Let the cake cool in the pan 10 minutes, then un-mold onto a wire rack and cool completely. Before serving, peel off the lining paper. Dust lightly with confectioners' sugar.

1 ▲ In a bowl, combine the eggs (at room temperature) and sugar. Set the bowl over a saucepan of simmering water; the base of the bowl should not touch the water.

2 ▲ Beat with a handheld electric mixer at medium-high speed until the mixture is very thick and pale, about 10 minutes.

3 ▲ Lift out the beaters; the mixture on the beaters should trail back onto the surface of the remaining mixture in the bowl to make a ribbon that holds it shape.

4 ▲ Remove the bowl from over the pan of water and continue beating until the mixture is cool, 2–3 minutes.

5 ▲ Sift the flour and fold it into the mixture, cutting in to the bottom of the bowl with a rubber spatula or large metal spoon, and turning the batter over, working gently yet thoroughly, to retain the volume of the egg and sugar mixture.

6 ▲ Pour the batter into the prepared pan or pans and bake as directed. To test if a spongecake is done, press the center lightly with your fingertip: the cake should spring back.

MAKING A JELLY ROLL

A rolled spongecake reveals an attractive swirl of filling when it is sliced. Some filling ideas are sweetened whipped cream, ice cream, fruit preserves, or butter frosting.

The spongecake batter can be made using whole or separated eggs.

Line the pan with either wax paper or baking parchment. Lightly grease the paper and dust with a little flour, shaking off any excess.

Chocolate Ice-Cream Roll
Make the spongecake batter using 4 eggs, separated, ⅔ cup sugar, and ⅔ cup cake flour sifted with 3 tablespoons unsweetened cocoa powder. Pour into a prepared 15- × 10-inch jelly roll pan. Bake in a preheated 375°F oven about 15 minutes. Turn out, roll up, and let cool. When cold, unroll the cake and spread with 2½ cups softened vanilla or chocolate ice cream. Roll up the cake again, wrap in foil, and freeze until firm. About 30 minutes before serving, transfer the cake to the refrigerator. Sprinkle with granulated or confectioners' sugar before serving. If desired, serve with warm bittersweet chocolate sauce. *Serves 6–8.*

1 ▲ Pour the batter into the prepared pan and spread it evenly into the corners with a metal spatula. Bake as directed in the recipe.

3 ▲ Carefully peel off the lining paper from the cake. If necessary, trim off any crisp crust from the side of the cake.

5 ▲ Remove the towel and unroll the cake. Lift off the paper. Spread the chosen filling over the cake.

2 ▲ Spread a dish towel flat and lay a sheet of parchment paper on top. Sprinkle the paper evenly as directed with granulated or confectioners' sugar, cocoa powder, or a spice mixture. Invert the cake onto the paper.

4 ▲ Carefully roll up the cake, with the paper inside, starting from a short side. Wrap the towel around the cake roll and let cool on a wire rack.

6 ▲ Roll the cake up again, using the paper to help move it forward. Sprinkle with sugar or frost, as the recipe directs.

PASTRY

~

Making light, crisp pastry needn't be difficult and the step-by-step pictures help achieve a good result every time. Various pastries are described; with techniques of handling pastry and how to decorate the finished product.

MAKING BASIC PIE PASTRY

A tender, flaky piecrust sets off any pie filling to perfection. The pastry dough here uses shortening, which makes a dough that is easy to roll out and line into pie plates. It is an excellent all-purpose pastry dough.

FOR A 9-INCH SINGLE-CRUST PIE

1¼ cups flour
¼ teaspoon salt
½ cup shortening
3–4 tablespoons ice water

Pastrymaking Tips

● A pastry blender works very well, but you can also use two knives, scissor-fashion, to cut the fat into the flour, or rub in the fat with your fingertips.

● It helps if the fat is cold and firm, particularly if making the dough in a food processor or if using butter for tart pastry. If the fat softens too much when being blended into the flour, the pastry may be oily.

● Liquids used in pastrymaking should be ice cold so that they will not melt the fat.

● When cutting or rubbing the fat into the flour, if it should begin to soften and feel oily, put the bowl in the refrigerator to chill 20–30 minutes, then continue.

● When adding the liquid, start with the smaller amount (added all at once, not in a dribble), and only add more if the mixture will not come together. Too much water will result in tough pastry.

● When gathering the mixture together into a ball of dough, handle it as little as possible; overworked pastry will not be tender.

● To avoid shrinkage, refrigerate the pastry dough before rolling out and baking.

1 ▲ Sift the flour and salt into a bowl. Add the shortening. Cut or rub it into the flour until it is in pieces the size of small peas.

3 ▲ Press the dough into a ball. If it is too dry to form a dough, add the remaining water.

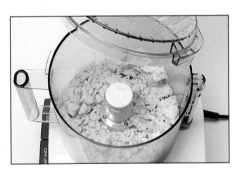

5 ▲ To make pastry in a food processor: Combine the flour, salt, and shortening in the work bowl. Process, turning the machine on and off, just until the mixture is crumbly. Add the ice water and process again briefly – just until the dough starts to pull away from the sides of the bowl. It should still look crumbly. Remove the dough from the processor bowl and gather it into a ball. Wrap and refrigerate.

2 ▲ Sprinkle 3 tablespoons water over the mixture. With a fork, toss gently to mix and moisten it.

4 ▲ Wrap the ball of dough with plastic wrap or wax paper and refrigerate at least 45 minutes.

Pastry Variations

● For *Whole-Wheat Pie Pastry*: Use 1 cup all-purpose flour and ⅓ cup whole-wheat flour. Increase the ice water to 4–5 tablespoons.

● For *Nut Pie Pastry*: Add ¼ cup finely chopped walnuts or pecans to the flour mixture.

● For *Spice Pie Pastry*: Sift 1 teaspoon cinnamon with the flour.

● For a *Double-Crust Pie*: Use 2¼ cups flour, ½ teaspoon salt, ¾ cup shortening, and 6–7 tablespoons ice water for basic pie pastry. (For nut or spice pastry, double the additions, using ½ cup finely chopped nuts added to the flour or 2 teaspoons cinnamon sifted with the flour.) Divide dough in half, shape into balls, and wrap separately.

MAKING TART PASTRY

The pastry for tarts and quiches is made mainly with butter, giving a rich and crumbly result. The more butter used, the richer the pastry will be – almost like a cookie dough – and the harder to roll out. If you have difficulty rolling out the pastry, you can just press it into the pan instead. Another way is to roll it out between sheets of plastic wrap for easier handling.

Tart pastry, like pie pastry, can be made by hand or in a food processor.

FOR A 9-INCH TART SHELL

1½ cups flour
½ teaspoon salt
6 tablespoons butter, chilled
3 tablespoons shortening
1 egg yolk
¼ teaspoon lemon juice
2–3 tablespoons ice water

1 ▲ Sift the flour and salt into a bowl. Add the butter and shortening. Cut or rub into the flour until the mixture resembles coarse meal.

2 ▲ In a small bowl, mix the egg yolk, lemon juice, and 2 tablespoons water. Add to the flour mixture. With a fork, toss gently to mix and moisten.

3 ▲ Press the dough into a rough ball. If it is too dry to come together, add the remaining water. Turn onto the work surface or a pastry board.

4 ▲ With the heel of your hand, push small portions of dough away from you, smearing them on the work surface.

Tart Pastry Variations
- For *Sweet Tart Pastry*: Reduce the amount of salt to ¼ teaspoon and add 1 tablespoon sugar, sifting it with the flour.
- For *Rich Tart Pastry*: Use 1½ cups flour, ½ teaspoon salt, 9 tablespoons butter, 2 egg yolks, and 1–2 tablespoons ice water.
- For *Rich Sweet Tart Pastry*: Make rich tart pastry, adding 3 tablespoons sugar with the flour and ½ teaspoon vanilla extract with the egg yolks.

5 ▲ Continue mixing the dough in this way until it feels pliable and can be peeled easily off the surface.

6 ▲ Press the dough into a smooth ball. Wrap with plastic wrap and refrigerate at least 2 hours.

ROLLING OUT AND LINING A PIE PLATE

A neat crust that doesn't distort or shrink in baking is the desired result. The key to success is handling the dough gently.

First remove the chilled dough from the refrigerator and let it soften slightly at room temperature. Unwrap and put it on a lightly floured surface. Flatten the dough into a neat, round disk. Sprinkle the top with a little flour. Lightly flour the rolling pin.

Rolling Out and Lining Tips

• A pastry cloth and a stockinette cover for your rolling pin will ensure that your pastry dough does not stick when rolling out.

• Reflour the surface and rolling pin if the dough starts to stick.

• Should the dough tear, patch the hole with a small piece of moistened dough.

• When rolling out and lining the pie plate, do not stretch the dough. It will only shrink back during baking, spoiling the shape of the pie shell.

• Once or twice during rolling out, gently push in the edges of the dough with your cupped palms, to keep the circular shape.

• A pastry scraper will help lift the dough from the work surface, to wrap it around the rolling pin.

• Pie plates made from heat-resistant glass or dull-finish metal such as heavyweight aluminum will give a crisp crust.

• When finishing the edge, be sure to hook the dough over the rim all the way around or to press the dough firmly to the rim. This will prevent the dough pulling away should it start to shrink slightly during baking.

• To prevent the edge of the pie-crust from overbrowning, cover it with foil. Remove the foil half-way through baking.

1 ▲ Using even pressure, start rolling out the dough, working from the center to the edge each time and easing the pressure slightly as you reach the edge.

3 ▲ Continue rolling out until the dough circle is about 2 inches larger all around than the pie plate. The dough will be about ⅛-inch thick.

5 ▲ Hold the pin over the pie plate and gently unroll the dough so it drapes into the plate, centering it as much as possible.

2 ▲ Lift up the dough and give it a quarter turn from time to time during the rolling. This will prevent the dough sticking to the surface, and will help keep the thickness even.

4 ▲ Set the rolling pin on the dough, near one side of the circle. Fold the outside edge of dough over the pin, then roll the pin over the dough to wrap the dough around it. Do this gently and loosely.

6 ▲ With your fingertips, ease the dough into the plate, gently pressing it smoothly over the bottom and up the side. With kitchen scissors or a knife, trim the dough according to the edge to be made.

FINISHING THE EDGE OF A PIE

1 ▲ For a fork-finished edge: Trim the dough even with the rim and press it flat. Firmly and evenly press the tines of a fork all around the edge. If the fork sticks, dip it in flour.

2 ▲ For a fluted or pinched edge: Trim the dough to leave a ½-inch overhang all around. Fold the extra dough under to build up the edge. Put the knuckle or tip of the index finger of one hand inside the edge, pointing directly out. With the thumb and index finger of your other hand, pinch the dough edge around your index finger into a "V" shape. Continue all the way around the edge.

3 ▲ For a ruffled or scalloped edge: Trim the dough to leave a ½-inch overhang all around. Fold the extra dough under to build up the edge. Hold the thumb and index finger of one hand 1 inch apart, inside the edge, pointing directly out. With the index finger of your other hand, gently pull the dough between them, to the end of the rim. Continue all the way around the edge.

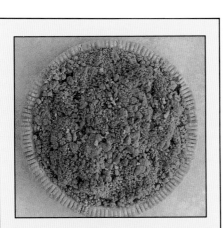

Apple and Cherry Streusel Pie
Mix together 3 cups peeled, cored, and sliced apples, 2 cups pitted tart red cherries, and ½ cup firmly packed light brown sugar. Put the fruit mixture into a 9-inch pie shell and spread out evenly. For the topping, combine ⅔ cup flour, ½ cup firmly packed brown sugar, and 1 teaspoon ground cinnamon. Cut in 6 tablespoons butter until the mixture resembles coarse crumbs. Sprinkle evenly over the fruit. Bake in a preheated 375°F oven until golden brown, about 45 minutes. *Serves 6.*

4 ▲ For a cutout edge: Trim the dough even with the rim of the pie plate and press it flat on the rim. With a small cookie cutter, cut out shapes from the dough trimmings. Moisten the edge of the pastry shell and press the cutouts in place, overlapping them slightly if desired.

5 ▲ For a ribbon edge: Trim the dough even with the rim of the pie plate and press it flat on the rim. Cut long strips, about ¾-inch wide, from the dough trimmings. Moisten the edge and press one end of a strip onto it. Twist the strip gently and press it onto the edge again. Continue all the way around the edge.

MAKING A DOUBLE-CRUST PIE

Two tender pastry layers enveloping a sweet filling – what could be nicer? It is easy to see why the double-crust pie is an American institution.

Apple Pie
Combine 6 cups peeled, cored, and thinly sliced apples, 1 tablespoon flour, ½ cup sugar, and ¾ teaspoon apple pie spice. Toss together until the fruit is evenly coated with the sugar and flour. Use to fill the pie (use spice pie pastry if desired). Bake in a preheated 375°F oven until the pastry is golden brown and the fruit is tender (test with a skewer through a slit in the crust), about 45 minutes. Cool on a rack.

1 ▲ Roll out half of the pastry dough on a floured surface and line a pie plate. Trim the dough even with the rim of the pie plate.

2 ▲ Put in the filling. Brush the edge of the pie shell evenly with water to moisten it.

3 ▲ Roll out a second piece of dough to a circle that is about 1 inch larger all around than the pie plate. Roll it up around the rolling pin and unroll it over the pie. Press the edges together.

4 ▲ Trim the edge of the top crust to leave a ½-inch overhang. Cut slits or a design in the center. These will act as steam vents during baking.

5 ▲ Fold the overhang under the edge of the bottom crust. Press the two crusts together gently and evenly to seal. Finish the edge, as desired.

6 ▲ Brush the top crust with milk or cream for a shiny finish. Or, brush with 1 egg yolk mixed with 1 teaspoon water for a glazed golden-brown finish. Or, brush with water and then sprinkle with sugar or cinnamon-sugar for a sugary crust.

7 ▲ If desired, cut out decorative shapes from the dough trimmings, rolled out as thinly as possible. Moisten the cutouts with a little water and press them onto the top crust. Glaze the decorations before baking.

MAKING A LATTICE TOP

A woven pastry lattice is a very attractive finish for a pie. Prepare pastry dough for a double-crust pie.

Roll out half of the pastry dough and line the pie plate. Trim the dough to leave a ½-inch overhang all around. Put in the filling. Roll out the second piece of dough into a circle that is about 2 inches larger all around than the pie plate.

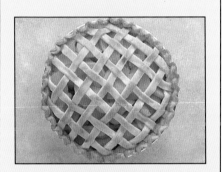

Apricot Lattice Pie
Combine 6 cups peeled, pitted, thinly sliced apricots, 2 tablespoons flour, and ½ cup sugar. Toss to coat the fruit evenly. Fill the pie shell and make a lattice top. Glaze with milk and bake in a preheated 375°F oven until the pastry is golden brown and the filling is bubbling, about 45 minutes. Cool on a wire rack.

1 ▲ With the help of a ruler, cut neat, straight strips of dough that are about ½-inch wide, using a knife or fluted pastry wheel.

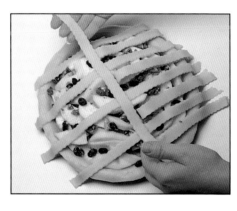

3 ▲ Fold back every other strip from the center. Lay another strip across the center, on the flat strips, at right angles to them. Lay the folded strips flat again.

5 ▲ Continue folding the strips in this way until half of the lattice is completed. Repeat on the other half of the pie.

2 ▲ **For a square woven lattice:** Lay half of the strips across the pie filling, keeping them neatly parallel and spacing them evenly.

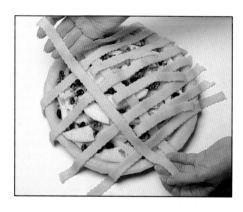

4 ▲ Now fold back those strips that were not folded the first time. Lay another strip across those that are flat now, spacing this new strip evenly from the center strip.

6 ▲ Trim the ends of the strips even with the rim of the pie plate. Moisten the edge of the bottom crust and press the strips gently to it to seal. Finish the edge.

7 ▲ **For a diamond lattice:** Weave as above, laying the intersecting strips diagonally instead of at right angles. Or, lay half the strips over the filling and the remaining strips on top.

LINING A TART PAN OR FLAN RING

A tart pan is shallow, with no rim. Its straight sides (smooth or fluted) give a tart or quiche the traditional shape. The most useful pans have removable bottoms, making it easy to unmold a tart. Flan rings, also called tart bands, are straight-sided metal rings that are set on a baking sheet. In addition to these, there are porcelain quiche dishes and small, individual tartlet tins or molds, both plain and fluted.

Pecan Tartlets
Line six 4-inch tartlet shells with tart pastry. Divide 1½ cups pecan halves among them. In a bowl, beat 3 eggs to mix. Add 2 tablespoons melted butter, 1 cup light corn syrup, and ½ teaspoon vanilla extract. In another bowl, sift together 1 cup sugar and 1 tablespoon flour. Add to the egg mixture and stir until evenly blended. Divide among the tartlet shells and let stand until the nuts rise to the surface. Bake in a preheated 350°F oven until a knife inserted in the filling near the center comes out clean, 35–40 minutes. Let cool on a wire rack before serving. *Makes 6.*

1 ▲ Remove the chilled dough from the refrigerator and let it soften slightly at room temperature. Roll out to a circle that is about 2 inches larger all around than the tart pan. It will be about ⅛-inch thick.

2 ▲ Roll up the dough around the rolling pin, then unroll it over the pan, draping it gently.

3 ▲ With your fingertips, ease the dough into the pan, gently pressing it smoothly over the bottom, without stretching it.

4 ▲ Fold the overhanging dough down inside the pan, to thicken the side of the pastry shell. Smooth and press the side of the shell against the side of the pan.

5 ▲ Roll the rolling pin over the top of the pan to cut off excess pastry dough. Smooth the cut edge and press it against the side of the pan, if necessary, to keep it in place.

6 ▲ For tartlet molds: Arrange them close together and unroll the dough over the molds, draping it loosely. Roll the rolling pin over the top to cut off excess pastry. Press into the bottom and sides of the molds.

BAKING A PASTRY SHELL WITHOUT A FILLING

Baked custard and cream fillings can make pastry soggy, so the shells for these pies and tarts are often prebaked before the filling is added and the final baking is done. Such prebaking is referred to as baking "blind." The technique is also used for pastry shells that are to be filled with an uncooked or precooked mixture.

The purpose of using weights is to prevent the bottom of the pastry shell from rising too much and becoming distorted, thus keeping its neat shape.

1 ▲ Set the pie plate, tart pan, or flan ring on a sheet of parchment paper or foil. Draw or mark around its base. Cut out a circle about 3 inches larger all around than the drawn or marked one.

2 ▲ Roll out the pastry dough and use to line the pie plate, tart pan, or flan ring set on a baking sheet. Prick the bottom of the pastry shell all over with a fork.

Fresh Strawberry Tart
Make the shell using sweet tart pastry or rich sweet tart pastry. Bake it "blind" and then let it cool. Combine 14 ounces cream cheese, ¼ cup sugar, 1 egg yolk, and ¼ cup whipping cream. Beat until smooth. Fold in 1 stiffly beaten egg white. Pour the mixture into the tart shell and spread it evenly. Bake at 350°F until the filling is softly set, 15–20 minutes; it will set further as it cools. Let cool. Arrange halved strawberries neatly over the surface in concentric circles. Heat ½ cup red currant jelly until it melts; brush it all over the berries to glaze them. Let cool and set before serving. *Serves 6.*

3 ▲ Lay the circle of parchment paper or foil in the pastry shell and press it smoothly over the bottom and up the side.

4 ▲ Put enough dried beans or pie weights in the shell to cover the bottom thickly.

5 ▲ For partially baked pastry: Bake the shell in a preheated 400°F oven until it is slightly dry and set, 15–20 minutes. Remove the paper or foil and beans. It is now ready to be filled and baked further.

6 ▲ For fully baked pastry: After baking 15 minutes, remove the paper or foil and beans. Prick the bottom again with a fork. Return to the oven and continue baking until golden brown, 5–10 minutes longer. Let cool completely before adding the filling.

CREAM-PUFF PASTRY

Unlike other pastries, where the fat is cut into the flour, with cream-puff pastry (also called choux pastry) the butter is melted with water and then the flour is added, followed by eggs. The result is more of a paste than a pastry. It is easy to make, but take care in measuring the ingredients.

FOR 18 SMALL PUFFS OR 12 ECLAIRS

1 stick (8 tablespoons) butter, cut into pieces
1 cup water
2 teaspoons sugar (optional)
¼ teaspoon salt
1 cup flour
4 eggs, beaten to mix

Shaping Cream-Puff Pastry
● For *large puffs*: Use two large spoons dipped in water (and your wet fingers, if necessary). Drop the paste in 2- or 2½-inch-wide blobs on the paper-lined baking sheet, leaving 1½–2 inches between each. Alternatively, for well-shaped puffs, pipe the paste using a pastry bag fitted with a ¾-inch plain tube.
● For *small puffs or profiteroles*: Use two small spoons or a pastry bag fitted with a ½-inch tube, and shape 1-inch-wide blobs.
● For *éclairs*: Use a pastry bag fitted with a ¾-inch plain tube. Pipe strips 4- to 5-inches long.
● For a *ring*: Draw a 12-inch circle on the parchment paper. Spoon the paste in large blobs on it. Or, pipe 2 rings on either side of the circle and a third ring on top.

Baking Cream-Puff Pastry
Large puffs and éclairs need 30–35 minutes, small puffs 20–25 minutes, rings 40–45 minutes.

1 ▲ Combine the butter, water, sugar, if using, and salt in a large heavy-based saucepan. Bring to a boil over medium-high heat, stirring occasionally to help melt the butter.

3 ▲ Return the pan to medium heat and cook, stirring, until the mixture will form a ball, pulling away from the side of the pan. This will take about 1 minute. Remove from the heat again and let cool 3–5 minutes.

5 ▲ While still warm, shape large cream puffs, éclairs, small puffs or profiteroles, or large rings on a baking sheet lined with parchment paper.

2 ▲ As soon as the mixture is boiling, remove the pan from the heat. Add the flour all at once and beat vigorously with a wooden spoon to mix the flour into the liquid.

4 ▲ Add a little of the beaten egg and beat well with the spoon or an electric mixer to incorporate. Add a little more egg and beat in well. Continue beating in the eggs until the mixture becomes a smooth, shiny paste thick enough to hold its shape.

6 ▲ Brush with an egg glaze made by beating 1 egg with 1 teaspoon cold water. Put into a preheated 425°F oven, then reduce the heat to 400°F. Bake until puffed and golden brown.

7 ▶ When baked (see baking times, left) make a slit in the side of each puff or éclair, or several around a ring, with the tip of a knife to let the steam inside escape. Return to the turned-off oven and dry out 5–10 minutes. Cool on a wire rack. Shortly before serving, split the pastries open horizontally and fill as desired.

Fillings for Cream-Puff Pastry
● Fill sweet puffs, éclairs, or profiteroles with sweetened whipped cream, or vanilla ice cream. Serve with bittersweet chocolate sauce.
● Fill savory puffs with egg salad or hot creamed chicken.

Hot Cheddar Puffs

MAKES ABOUT 28 APPETIZER PUFFS

4 tablespoons butter, cut into pieces

1 cup water

½ teaspoon salt

1 cup flour

¼ teaspoon mustard powder

⅛ teaspoon hot paprika

½ cup grated sharp Cheddar cheese

4 eggs, beaten

1 egg, beaten with 1 teaspoon cold water, for glazing

FOR THE FILLING

½ pound cream cheese, at room temperature

2 tablespoons smooth, spicy fruit sauce

¼ cup diced canned pimiento

2 tablespoons chopped black or green olives

1 Preheat the oven to 425°F.

2 Make the cream-puff pastry, adding the mustard and paprika with the flour and beating in the cheese before the eggs. Shape into small puffs on a baking sheet lined with parchment paper. Brush with the egg glaze.

3 Put them in the oven and immediately reduce the temperature to 400°F. Bake until risen, golden brown, and crisp, 20–25 minutes.

4 ▲ Meanwhile, for the filling, beat the cream cheese with the spicy fruit sauce until well blended. Mix in the pimiento and olives.

5 Cut a slit in the side of each puff and return to the turned-off oven to dry out about 10 minutes.

6 ▼ While the puffs are still warm, fill them with the cheese filling, piping or spooning it carefully into the slit cut in the side of each puff. Serve warm.

INDEX

~